I0101071

Dr. Bhavna Verma

Tribal Women in Jharkhand

Problems and Perspectives

CANADIAN

Academic Publishing

2015

Tribal Women in Jharkhand

Problems and Perspectives

Dr. Bhavna Verma

(MSW, Ph.D.)

Associate Professor

Department of Social Work

Mahatma Gandhi Kashi Vidyapith

Varanasi, Uttar Pradesh (India)

CANADIAN

Academic Publishing

2015

Copyright © 2015. Dr. Bhavna Verma

All rights reserved. This book or any portion thereof may not be reproduced or used in any manner whatsoever without the express written permission of the publisher except for the use of brief quotations in a book review or scholarly journal.

Price : $27.86

First Edition : 2015

ISBN : 978-1-926488-11-0

ISBN Allotment Agency : Library and Archives Canada (Govt. of Canada)

Published & Printed by
Canadian Academic Publishing
81, Woodlot Crescent,
Etobicoke,
Toronto, Ontario, Canada.
Postal Code- M9W 6T3
Phone- +1 (647) 633 9712
http://www.canadapublish.com

ACKNOWLEDGEMENT

The realities of rural life in India are difficult to comprehend. A majority of village do not have sustainable economics. In case of tribal society the tribal has their own culture and tradition. It is well recognised that the status of tribal women in a tribal society is better than that of their non-tribal counterparts. The tribal women are generally not perceived to have any meaningful income generation capacity, and hence, they are neglected mainly to houseful duties and cheap labour. Even in matter of sex (except in some tribal society) and child bearing, tribal women often do not have the ability to oppose the wishes of their men. It is the time that the role of growing poverty and deprivation in large areas is particularly highlighted.

I sincerely feel that is my responsibility to express my gratitude to each and everyone who has supported me in one way or other in the completing the project.

I shall be failing in my duties if I do not express my thanks to University Grants Commission, New Delhi for providing me an opportunity for conducting research project on "Socio-Economic Status of Tribes of State Jharkhand with Special Reference to women". The project is conducted in the two tribal concentrated blocks Chiniya and Bhandariya under Garhwa district of Jharkhand state.

Our respondents co-operated me and helped me in many ways. So I remember each of them with gratitude. And I thanks to officers of Tribal Welfare Research Institute, Ranchi, and Block Development Officers and Gram Sevek for providing information related to tribal communities.

I express my heartfelt thanks to Prof. Laxmi Dubey (Dean,Department of Social Work for her constant support and encouragement. I am thankful to Mr. S. L. Dubey (Retd.IAS Officer) for giving me valuable suggestion. I am grateful to Retd. Prof. Kazi Abdul Hadi, S.S.J.M. Namdhari College, Garhwa,Jharkhand and my cute kids Bhoutik and Bhavya who morally supported me. I express my thanks to Project Fellow Ms. Priyanka Tripathi, and I specially thanks to Mr. Maninder Deesuja, Ms. Deepika Mourya for their constant support and help without them project could not be reached at its final stage.

Dr. Bhavna Verma
Associate Professor
Department of Social Work,
Mahatma Gandhi Kashi Vidyapith
Varanasi, Uttar Pradesh (India)

CONTENTS

LIST OF TABLES

LIST OF TABLES

LIST OF TABLES

LIST OF TABLES

LIST OF FIGURES

CHAPTER – I
STATUS OF TRIBAL IN INDIA

Meaning of Tribe

Societies are made up of people and they have boundaries. It should also be noted that a society includes within itself various sub-systems and is not itself subsumed under any wider category. In other words, a society is a self-contained unit and its boundaries demarcate certain limits of interaction in the legal, political, economic and other spheres. This, of course, does not mean that no interaction takes place across the boundaries of different societies. However, the interaction existing among the members of a society has a distinct character. Thus, tribe may be defined as a collection of individuals generally living in isolation and sharing a common culture. The term 'culture' as used here denotes those traditional beliefs, arts, life styles and practices, which an individual acquires as a member of a particular society.

Oxford Illustrated Dictionary (1963:886) defines tribe as 'a group of primitive or barbarous clans under recognised chiefs'. However, this does not happen to reflect all characteristics of a tribe. Theodorson and Theodorson (1969:443) in" A Modern Dictionary of Sociology" define 'tribe' as follows: 'In most usage, a non-literate community or a collection of such communities occupying a common geographic area and having a similar language and culture'. Piddington (1963:64) says that 'a tribe is a group of people speaking a common dialect, inhabiting a common territory and displaying certain homogeneity in their culture'. Hoebel (1949:513) opines that 'a tribe is a social group speaking 'a distinctive language or dialect and possessing a distinctive culture that makes it off from other tribes. It is not necessarily organized politically'. Taylor (1988:546) in his 'Dictionary of Anthropology' defines tribe as 'a social group, usually with a definite area, dialect, cultural homogeneity, and unifying social organization. It may include several sub-groups, such as, sibs or villages. A tribe ordinarily has a leader and may have a common ancestor as well as a patron deity. 'The families or small communities making up the tribe are linked through economic, social, religious, family or blood ties.

1

Majumdar (1958) defines a tribe as "a social group with territorial affiliation, endogamous, with no specialization of functions, ruled by tribal officers, hereditarily or otherwise, united in a language or dialect, recognizing social distance with other tribes or castes without any social obloquy attaching to them as it does in the caste structure, following tribal traditions, beliefs and customs, illiberal of naturalization of ideas from alien sources, above all conscious of homogeneity of ethnic and territorial integration."

To conclude, tribe may be defined as 'a group of people speaking a common language, observing uniform rules of social organization, and working together for common purposes such as trade, agriculture or warfare. They may also possess a common name, a contiguous territory, a relatively uniform culture or way of life, and a tradition of common descent' (Verma, 1996:3).

Thus in Indian context, they are commonly designated as *Adivasi* (original settlers), *Girijan* (hill dwellers), *Vanya jati* (forest caste men), *Adimjati* (Primitive castes), and *Anusuchit Janjati* (Scheduled tribes). The tribes of India who are unable to defend them and were gradually forced to recede before the invading hoards of such people, as the Dravidian, Indo-Aryans and Mongolians coming from the West, North West and North East. These people took shelter in the forest and mountain ranges. Those who were left behind in the plains generally disappeared either by absorption or by a culturalization.

Main Features of Tribes

The original tribes in India have been divided and sub-divided into large number of sub-tribes. They are mutually exclusive, each having the endogenous and exogamous clan with their own names and culture, customs, location practice and lifestyle. A well established criterion being followed is based on certain attributes such as:

- Geographical isolation: They live in cloister, exclusive remote and inhospitable areas like hills and forests

- Backwardness: Livelihood based on primitive agriculture, low cost closed economy based on low level of technology which caused poverty. They have a low level of literacy and poor health
- Distinctive culture, language and religion: They have developed community wise their own distinctive culture, language and religion
- Shyness of contact: They have margin degree of contact with other cultures and people

The Commissioner of Scheduled Castes and Scheduled Tribes, in its reports (1952) has listed eight features of the tribal groups in India:

- They live always away from the civilized world and are found in the inaccessible parts lying in the forest and hills.
- They generally belong to three stocks such as Negritos, Australoids and Mangoloids.
- They speak the same tribal dialect.

They prefer primitive occupations such as gleaning, hunting and gathering forest produce.

- They are mostly carnivorous.
- They live and prefer to be naked and semi-naked.
- They have nomadic habit and are fond of drinking and dancing.
- They prefer primitive religion known as "Animist" in which they worship ghost and spirits as the most important elements.

All the qualities are related to great extent, in a particular groups and villages of tribal India. But the qualities present in them differ in degree. Like other societies, tribal society is also not static, rather quite dynamic, but the rate of change in tribal society is very slow. That is why they have been backward and poor in comparison to other people. Since they have been materially backward and economically poor, attempts have been made by the Government their development. Today the government of almost all countries of the world is paying special attention towards the development of the tribal, i.e., one finds the existence of induced or planned change in tribal society.

Safeguards for Scheduled Tribes in Constitution

With the dawn of Independence and adoption of the Constitution of free India, the British policy of isolation and non-interference was replaced by a policy of integration through development. The Constitution of India has provided a number of safeguards for the welfare and development of the tribal. The relevant articles can be classified under four major heads: (a) Protective Provisions (Arts. 15, 16, 19, 46, 146, 342, etc.); (b) Developmental Provisions (Arts. 46, 275, etc.); (c) Administrative Provisions (Arts. 244 & 275) and (d) Reservation Provisions (Arts. 330, 332, 334, 335, 340, etc.). The Protective Provisions safeguard tribal people from social injustices and all forms of exploitation, while the Developmental Provisions promote with special care of educational and economic interests of the weaker sections like the Scheduled Tribes and Scheduled Castes. The Administrative Provisions under the Fifth and Sixth Schedules give special powers to the States *for the protection and governance of tribal areas* and the Reservation Provisions ensure due representation of the Scheduled tribes and Scheduled castes in legislative bodies and government jobs. The salient provisions of different articles are:

1. Article 244(1): Provisions as to the administration and control of Scheduled Areas and Scheduled Tribes.

2. Article 244(2): Provisions as to the administration of Tribal Areas.

3. Article 339: Control of the Union over the administration of Scheduled Areas and the welfare of the Scheduled Tribes.

4. Article 275(1): Provision for payment of grant-in-aid to enable the states to meet the cost of such development schemes as may be undertaken by the states with the approval of the Government of India for the purpose of promoting the welfare of the Scheduled Tribes in that State or raising the level of administration of the Scheduled Areas there in to that of the administration of the rest of the areas of that State.

5. Article 342: Specifying the tribes or tribal communities as Scheduled Tribes.

6. Article 330: Reservation of seats for the Scheduled Tribes in the House of the People.

7. Article 332: Reservation of seats for the Scheduled Tribes in the State Legislative Assemblies.

8. Article 334: Reservation of seats and special representation to cease after sixty year.

9. Article 164(1): In the States of Bihar, Madhya Pradesh and Orissa, there shall be a Minister in charge of tribal welfare who may in addition be in charge of the welfare of the Scheduled Castes and Backward Classes or any other work. (Now applicable to Chhattisgarh, Jharkhand, Madhya Pradesh and Orissa).

10. Article 338: There shall be a National Commission for the Scheduled Tribes and Scheduled Castes to be appointed by the Honourable President of India. (Since bifurcated into two, one for Scheduled Tribes and the other for Scheduled Castes).

11. Article 335: Claims of Scheduled Tribes to services and posts.

12. Article 46 Promotion of educational and economic interests of the Scheduled tribes, Scheduled castes and other weaker sections.

13. Article 371A: Special provision with reference to Nagaland.

14. Fifth Schedule: Provisions as to the Administration and control of Scheduled Areas.

15. Sixth Schedule: Provisions as to the Administration of Tribal Areas.

In addition to the above constitutional provisions, there are numbers of laws both Central and State, which provide protection and safeguards for the interest of the Scheduled tribes. These Acts and Regulations emanate from various constitutional provisions. Some of the important central Acts are as follows;

1. Protection of civil right Act, 1955

2. Forest Conservation Act, 1980

3. Bonded Labour (Prohibition and Regulation) Act, 1986

4. Child Labour (Prohibition and Regulation) Act, 1986

5. Scheduled Castes and Scheduled Tribes (Prevention of Atrocities) Act, 1989

6. The Provisions of the PESA (Panchayat Extension to Scheduled Areas) Act, 1996

7. The Schedule Tribes and other Traditional Forest Dwellers (Recognition of Forest Rights) Act, 2006 Similarly, State Governments safeguard for Tribal Development are related to the prevention of alienation and restoration of tribal land, money lending, reservations and so on.

The Constitution and Scheduled Areas

Unlike other communities the tribal people live in contiguous areas. It is, therefore, much simpler to have an area approach for development activities as well as regulatory provisions to protect their interests. In order to protect their interests; with regard to land and other social issues, various provisions have been enshrined in the Fifth Schedule of the Constitution. The Fifth Schedule under Article 244 (1) of the Constitution defines *"Scheduled Areas' as such areas as the "President may by order declare to be Scheduled Areas after consultation with the Governor of that State"*. The concept of Scheduled Area emerged during Fifth Five Year plan which is defined under Article 244(1) and Article 244(2). The Scheduled Area has been framed to protect the interest of Scheduled Tribes with regard to their land and other social issues. The history of Scheduled Area is very old and goes back to pre-British rule.

1. The history of Scheduled Areas can be traced from 1874, in which the British Government had introduced Scheduled District Act to provide administration in Scheduled districts.

2. According to the Scheduled District Act, Special Officers were appointed in the Scheduled Districts to look into the matter related to civil and criminal cases and to provide justice to the inhabitants of the area.

3. Attempt was made to collect taxes for providing better administration in the area.

4. In this Act, there was provision to extend the Scheduled Areas.

5. In the year 1919, the British Government introduced another Act, the tribal areas coming under the jurisdiction of Scheduled District Areas, were made free from legal boundary.

6. The tribal areas coming under Scheduled District areas were divided into two

categories: (i) Fully Excluded Areas and (ii) Corrected Excluded Areas.

7. Again through the Act 1935, Tribal areas were brought under the rule of Governor, appointed by the Honourable President of India and these areas were not brought under the rule of Parliament & State Assemblies.

8. At the time of Independence, the Constituent Assembly had paid *special attention towards the problem of tribal communities and the tribal areas.*

9. Therefore, the Scheduled Areas are nothing but another name of "Excluded and Partially Excluded Areas".

Creation of Scheduled Areas

For creating Scheduled Areas, the following objectives were kept in mind:

1. To assist the tribes with average interference and through small processor.

2. To develop the Scheduled Areas and to protect the interest of the tribes in the Areas.

Schedule Area Administration

According to 5th Schedule, the administration of Scheduled Areas as per Article 244 of the Constitution consists of following parts: a) Special Privilege to Governors b) Reports of Governors to the President of India and c) Tribes Advisory Council (TAC) According to Section "C" Para X of 5th Scheduled, the Scheduled Areas include those areas which have been 'Scheduled' by Hon'ble President of India. The President may amend the Scheduled Areas after discussing the problems with the concerned Governor of the State. The *Parliament may also make amendment of the Schedule Areas, but this will not be understood as Constitutional amendment.*

The Scheduled Areas are contagious areas traditionally conforming territorial units. In order to protect the interest of the Scheduled tribes and give them a special treatment, some of them have been put under the 5th Scheduled of the Constitution of India. The criteria for declaring any Scheduled Areas, which have a viable administrative entity such as; District, Block or Taluk and is the economy backwardness of the area.

The States covered under the 5th Scheduled Areas are 1) Orissa, 2) Andhra Pradesh, 3) Himachal Pradesh, 4) Gujarat, 5) Rajasthan 6) Maharashtra, 7) Bihar (now *Jharkhand has been declared after being separated from Bihar State)*, 8) Madhya Pradesh and 9) Chhattisgarh *(earlier Chhattisgarh was a part of undivided Madhya Pradesh State).*

The 6th Scheduled Areas under Article 244 (2) and 275 of the Constitution are those areas in the North-Eastern States like: 1) Assam, 2) Meghalaya, 3) Mizoram, 4) Arunachal Pradesh, 5) Manipur, 6) Nagaland and 7) Tripura, which have been declared as Tribal Areas *where provisions are made for the administration through Autonomous Districts/ Regional Councils.*

Comparative status of Scheduled Areas of different states under Fifth Scheduled:

The Scheduled Areas in the composite State of Bihar were originally specified by the Scheduled Areas (part A State) Order, 1950, (Constitution Order, 9) dated 23.01.1950 and there after they had been re-specified by the Scheduled Areas (State of Bihar, Gujarat, Madhya Pradesh and Orissa) Order 1977 (Constitution Order, 109) dated 31.12.1977 after rescinding the Order cited first so far as that related to the State of Bihar. Consequent upon formation of new State of Jharkhand vide Bihar Reorganization Act, 2000, the Scheduled Areas which were specified in relation to the composite State of Bihar stood transferred to the newly formed State of Jharkhand.

The Scheduled Areas of Jharkhand have been specified by the Scheduled Areas (State of Chhattisgarh, Jharkhand, and Madhya Pradesh) dated 20.2.2003 after receiving the Order dated 31.12.77 so far that related to the State of Bihar. The Scheduled Areas of Jharkhand specified with Scheduled Areas (State of Chhattisgarh, Jharkhand, and Madhya Pradesh) Order, 2003 (Constitution Order, 192) have rescinded vide Scheduled Areas (State of Jharkhand) Order, 2007(C.O.229) dated 11.4.2007.

Map 1: Map of India indicating States under Fifth and Sixth Scheduled

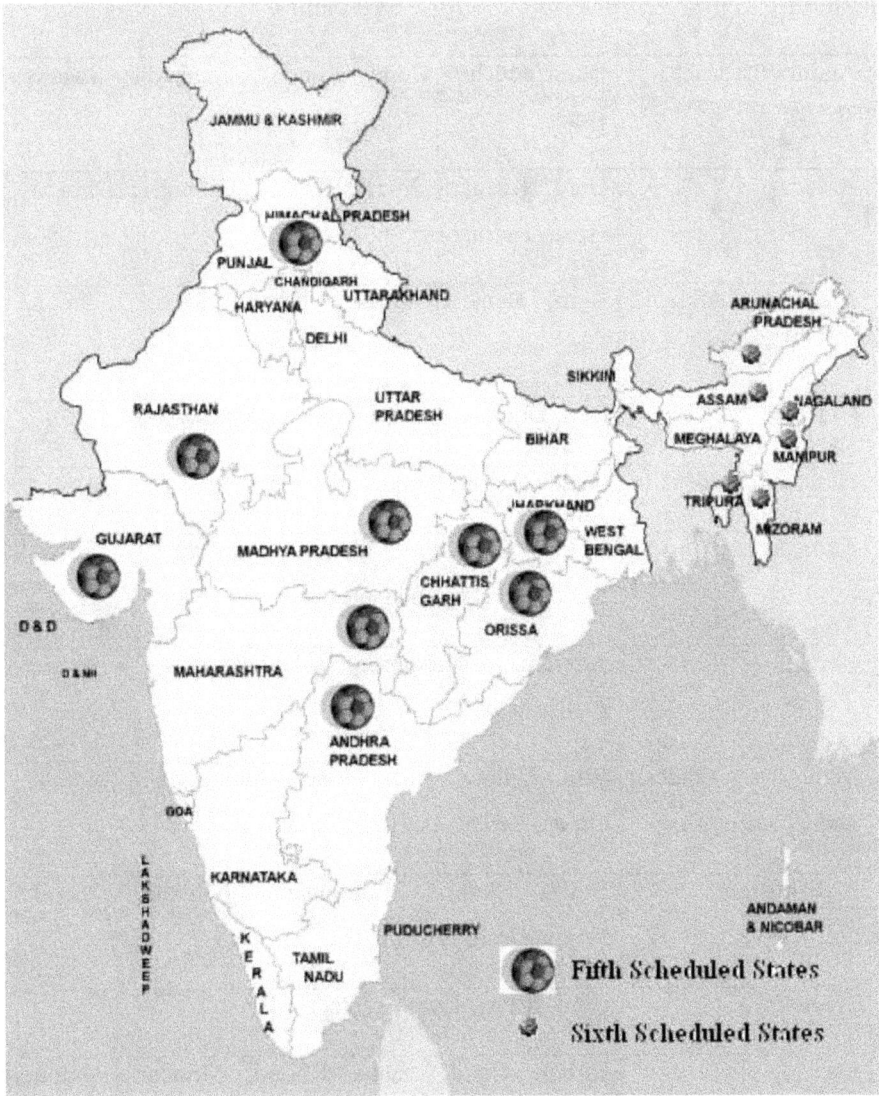

9

Table : 01.01

The Major Tribes in India

States	Tribes
Andhra Pradesh	Bhil,Chenchu, Gond, Kondas, Lambadis, Sugalis etc.
Assam	Boro, Kachari, Mikir (Karbi), Lalung, , Dimasa, Hmar, Hajong etc.
Bihar and Jharkhand	Asur, Banjara, Birhor, Korwa, Munda, Oraon, Santhal etc.
Gujarat	Bhil, Dhodia, Gond, Siddi, Bordia, etc.
Himachal Pradesh	Gaddi, Gujjar, Lahuala, Swangla, etc.
Karnataka	Bhil, Chenchu, Goud, Kuruba, , Kolis, Koya,Mayaka, Toda, etc.
Kerala	Adiyam, Kammrar, Kondkappus, Malais, Palliyar,etc
Madhya Pradesh and Chhatisgarh	Bhil, Birhor, Damar, Gond, Kharia, Majhi, Munda, Oraon, Parahi, etc.
Maharashtra	Bhil, Bhunjia, Chodhara, Dhodia, Gond, Kharia,Oraon, Pardhi, etc.
Meghalaya	Garo, Khasi, Jayantia, etc.
Orissa	Birhor, Gond, Juang, Khond, Mundari, Oraon, Santhal, Tharua, etc.
Rajasthan	Bhil, Damor, Garasta, Meena, Salariya etc.

Tamilnadu	Irular, Kammara, Kondakapus, Kota, Mahamalasar, Palleyan,Toda etc.
Tripura	Chakma, Garo, Khasi, Kuki, Lusai, Liang, Santhal etc.
West Bengal	Asur, Birhor, Korwa, Lepcha, Munda, Santhal, etc.
Mizoram	Lusai, Kuki, Garo, Khasi, Jayantia, Mikir etc.
Arunachal Pradesh	Dafla, Khampti, Singpho etc.
Goa	Dhodi, Siddi (Nayaka)
Daman and Diu	Dhodi, Mikkada, Varti, etc.
Andaman and Nicobar **Islands**	Jarawa, Nicobarese, Onges, Sentinelese, Shompens, Great Andamanese
Dadra and Nagar Haveli	As in Daman and Diu
Uttar Pradesh and Uttaranchal	Bhoti, Buxa, Jaunsari, Tharu, Raji etc
Nagaland	Naga, Kuki, Mikir, Garo, etc.
Sikkim	Bhutia, Lepcha etc
Jammu and Kashmir	Chdddangpa, Garra, Gujjar, Gaddi, etc.

Source: Annual Report, 2000-2001, Ministry of Tribal Affairs, Govt. of India

Table : 01.02

Distribution of STs Population in different States/Uts

S. No.	State/UTs	% of ST Population in States/UTs to the Total ST Population of the Country
1	Madhya Pradesh	14.51
2	Maharashtra	10.17
3	Orissa	9.66
4	Gujarat	8.87
5	Rajasthan	8.42
6	Jharkhand	8.40
7	Chhattisgarh	7.85
8	Andhra Pradesh	5.96
9	West Bengal	5.23
10	Karnataka	4.11
11	Assam	3.92
12	Meghalaya	2.36
13	Nagaland	2.10
14	Jammu and Kashmir	1.31
15	Tripura	1.18
16	Mizoram	1.00

17	Bihar	0.90
18	Manipur	0.88
19	Arunachal Pradesh	0.84
20	Tamil Nadu	0.77
21	Kerala	0.43
22	Uttaranchal	0.30
23	Himachal Pradesh	0.29
24	Dadra and Nagar Haveli	0.16
25	Sikkim	0.13
26	Uttar Pradesh	0.13

Source: Census of India, 2001

Tribal Population in India

The tribes are children of nature. They occupy around 18.7 percent of the total geographical area of the country. According to 1991 Census, the population of Scheduled Tribes in the country was 67758380, constituting about 8.08 per cent of the total population According to 2001 Census, the population of Scheduled Tribes in the country was 84,326,240, constituting about 8.20 per cent of the total population. In Orissa the population of Scheduled Tribes was 8,145,081 (22.13%) of the state total population. The tribal population in India is unevenly distributed in different States/Union territories, except in the state like Hariyana, Punjab, Chandigarh, Delhi and Pondichery. It is reflected well in the data presented in table 4 (figure I). State wise, Madhya Pradesh accounts for the highest percentage of Scheduled Tribes population to total STs population of the country (14.5 %) followed by Maharashtra (10.2 %), Orissa (9.7 %), Gujarat (8.9 %), Rajasthan (8.4 %), Jharkhand (8.4 %) and

Chhattisgarh (7.8 %). In fact, 68 per cent of the country's Scheduled Tribes population lives in these seven States. The proportion of the Scheduled Tribes to the total population of the States/Union territories is highest in Mizoram (94.5 %) and Lakshadweep (94.5 %) followed by Nagaland (89.1 %), Meghalaya (85.9 %). Within the major states Chhattisgarh (31.8%) has the highest percentage of Scheduled Tribes population followed by Jharkhand (26.3%) and Orissa (22.1%). These proportions are lowest in Uttar Pradesh (0.1 %), Bihar (0.9 %), Tamilnadu (1.0 %) and Kerala (1.1%). Out of their total population in the country, 91.7 per cent were living in rural areas, whereas, only 8.3 per cent from urban areas. The sex ratio of Scheduled Tribes population was 978 females per thousand males. The sex ratio among Scheduled Tribes population is higher than that of the total population of the country as well as that of SCs.

Table : 01.03

Number of Scheduled tribes Notified in States and Union Territories, 1991

S. No.	State/Union Territory	No. of Scheduled Tribes
	India	573
	States	---
1	Andhra Pradesh	33
2	Arunachal Pradesh	12
3	Assam	14
4	Bihar	30
5	Goa	05
6	Gujarat	29
7	Himachal Pradesh	08
8	Jammu and Kashmir	08
9	Karnataka	49
10	Kerala	35
11	Madhya Pradesh	46
12	Maharashtra	47
13	Manipur	29

14

14	Meghalaya	17
15	Mizoram	14
16	Nagaland	05
17	Orissa	62
18	Rajasthan	12
19	Sikkim	02
20	Tamil Nadu	36
21	Tripura	19
22	Uttar Pradesh	05
23	West Bengal	38
	Union Territories	
1	Andaman and Nicobar Island	06
2	Dadra and Nagar Haveli	07
3	Daman and Diu	05
4	Lakshadweep	*

Source: Census of India, 1991, Series I, Paper 2 of the 1992, P.38

* Inhabitants of Lakshadweep who, and both of whose parents, were born in Lakshadweep have been treated as Scheduled Tribes.

The tribal population is increasing along with the Indian population but at a rate lower than that of general population. This indicates that there is no systematic persecution though there may be exploitation. The growth in the tribal population during the last 50 years has been set out at table 6. The decennial growth rates are significantly lower than the average general population growth. The general population from 1951 to 2001 has increased by 667.51 millions. The ST population from 1951 to 2001 increased by 65.2 millions. The percentage of ST population to total population has increased only 2.91 per cent from 1951 to 2001.

Table : 01.04

Distribution ST Population from 1951 to 2001

(In Millions)

Year	Schedule Tribes	General Population	% of ST to Total Population
1951	19.1	361.1	5.29
1961	30.1	439.2	6.85
1971	38.0	548.2	6.93
1981	51.6	685.2	7.53
1991	67.8	846.3	8.10
2001	84.3	1028.61	8.20

Source: Annual Report 2007-08, Ministry of Tribal Affair, Government of India

The details of distribution of the districts in terms of concentration of ST population are given below:

In a little over half of the total number of 543 districts, STs accounted for less than 5% of the total population. On the other hand, in 75 districts the share of STs to total population was 50 per cent or higher. In the state of Haryana, Punjab, Chandigarh, Delhi and Pondichery, no Scheduled Tribe is notified. Concentration of ST population across district is given in table 7. In majority of the districts (i.e., 403 districts), the concentration of STs Population to its total population is less than 20 per cent.

Map 2 State wise Percentage of Scheduled Tribe Population in India as per 2001 Census

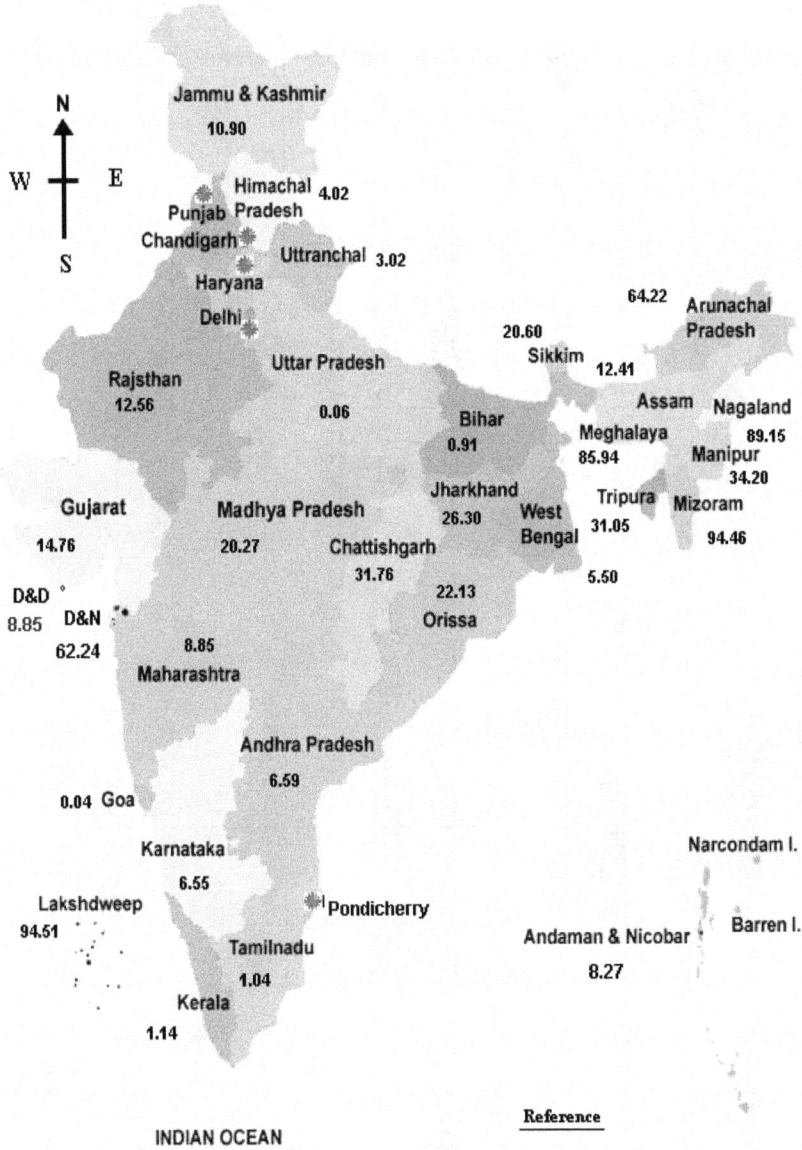

N
W ─── E
S

Jammu & Kashmir
10.90

Himachal 4.02
Punjab Pradesh
Chandigarh
Uttranchal 3.02
Haryana
Delhi
Uttar Pradesh
0.06

Rajsthan
12.56

64.22 Arunachal
Pradesh

20.60
Sikkim
12.41

Bihar
0.91

Assam Nagaland
Meghalaya 89.15
85.94 Manipur
34.20

Jharkhand
26.30 West
Bengal
31.05

Tripura Mizoram
94.46

Gujarat
14.76

Madhya Pradesh
20.27 Chattishgarh
31.76

22.13
Orissa

5.50

D&D °
8.85 D&N
62.24

8.85
Maharashtra

Andhra Pradesh
6.59

0.04 Goa

Karnataka
6.55

Lakshdweep
94.51

Pondicherry

Narcondam I.

Andaman & Nicobar
8.27

Barren I.

Tamilnadu
1.04
Kerala
1.14

INDIAN OCEAN

Reference

No ST Population

Found in the states/UTs of Punjab,
Haryana, Delhi, Chandigarh and Pondicherry

17

Table : 01.05

Percentage of Scheduled Tribe Population by India/state.

State / UT	Total Population		Decadal Growth Rate	ST Population		Decadal Growth Rate	% of STs in the State to total state population	% of STs in the State to total ST population
	1991	2001		1991	2001	2001		
India	838,583,988	1,028,610,328	22.66	67,758,380	84,326,240	24.45	8.20	8.20
Andhra Pradesh	66,508,008	76,210,007	14.59	4,199,481	5,024,104	19.64	6.59	6.59
Arunachal Pradesh	864,558	1,097,968	27.00	550,351	705,158	28.13	64.22	64.22
Assam	22,414,322	26,655,528	18.92	2,874,441	3,308,570	15.10	12.41	12.41
Bihar	86,374,465	82,998,509	-	6,616,914	758,351	-	0.91	0.91
Chhattisgarh		20,833,803	-		6,606,596	-	31.76	31.76
Goa	1,169,793	1,347,668	15.21	376	566	50.53	0.04	0.04
Gujarat	41,309,582	50,671,017	22.66	6,161,775	7,481,160	21.41	14.76	14.76
Haryana	16,463,648	21,144,564	28.43	NST	NST	NST	NST	NST
Himachal Pradesh	5,170,877	6,077,900	17.54	218,349	244,587	12.02	4.02	4.02

Jharkhand		29,945,829	-		7,087,068	-	26.30	26.30
Karnataka	44,977,201	52,850,562	17.51	1,915,691	3,463,986	80.82	6.55	6.55
Kerala	29,098,518	31,841,374	9.43	320,967	364,189	13.47	1.14	1.14
Madhya Pradesh	66,181,170	60,348,023	-	15,399,034	12,233,474	-	20.27	20.27
Maharashtra	78,937,187	96,878,627	22.73	7,318,281	8,577,276	17.20	8.85	8.85
Manipur	1,837,149	2,166,788	17.94	632,173	741,141	17.24	34.20	34.20
Meghalaya	1,774,778	2,318,822	30.65	1,517,927	1,992,862	31.29	85.94	85.94
Mizoram	689,756	888,573	28.82	653,565	839,310	28.42	94.46	94.46
Nagaland	1,209,546	1,990,036	64.53	1,060,822	1,774,026	67.23	89.15	89.15
Orissa	31,659,736	36,804,660	16.25	7,032,214	8,145,081	15.83	22.13	22.13
Punjab	20,281,969	24,358,999	20.10	NST	NST	NST	NST	NST
Rajasthan	44,005,990	56,507,188	28.41	5,474,881	7,097,706	29.64	12.56	12.56
Sikkim	406,457	540,851	33.06	90,901	111,405	22.56	20.60	20.60
Tamil Nadu	55,858,946	62,405,679	11.72	574,194	651,321	13.43	1.04	1.04

Tripura	2,757,205	3,199,203	16.03	853,345	993,426	16.42	31.05	31.05
Uttaranchal		8,489,349	-		256,129	-	3.02	3.02
Uttar Pradesh	139,112,287	166,197,921	19.47	2,87,901	107,963	-	0.06	0.06
West Bengal	68,077,965	80,176,197	17.77	3,808,760	4,406,794	15.70	5.50	5.50
Andaman & Nicobar Isl.	280,661	356,152	26.90	26,770	29,469	10.08	8.27	8.27
Chandigarh	642,015	900,635	40.28	NST	NST	NST	NST	NST
Dadra &Nagar Haveli	138,477	220,490	59.22	109,380	137,225	25.46	62.24	62.24
Daman and Diu	101,586	158,204	55.73	11,724	13,997	19.39	8.85	8.85
Delhi	9,420,644	13,850,507	47.02	NST	NST	NST	NST	NST
Laksadweep	51,707	60,650	17.30	48,163	57,321	19.01	94.51	94.51
Pondicherry	807,785	974,345	20.62	NST	NST	NST	NST	NST
Jammu and Kashmir		10,143,700	-		1,105,979	-	10.90	10.90

S urce: Census of India, 2001. *S urce:* Annual Report 2007-2008, Ministry of Tribal Affair, GoI

The decadal growth rate between 1961-1971 and 1991-2001 is almost at par rate with the general population of our country that i.e., ST growth rate is about 2 per cent higher. But during 1971-81 and 1981-91 the growth rate of ST is significantly much higher i.e., about 8.5 per cent than the counterpart.

Sex Ratio of Scheduled Tribe

Another feature of the population composition with particular reference to women, which can be studied with the available census data, is sex ratio (females per 1,000 males). A notable feature in this regard is that among the States and UTs with a sex ratio of more than 900, the highest ratio is observed among the scheduled tribes. As given in the Figure III, the sex ratio of Scheduled tribes in 2001 is much higher than the average sex ratio of the country. In 2001 census the sex ratio for scheduled tribe was 978 where as it was 933 for general population. The sex ratio for general population shows a declining trend.

Figure III: Sex Ratio of Scheduled Tribes and Total population

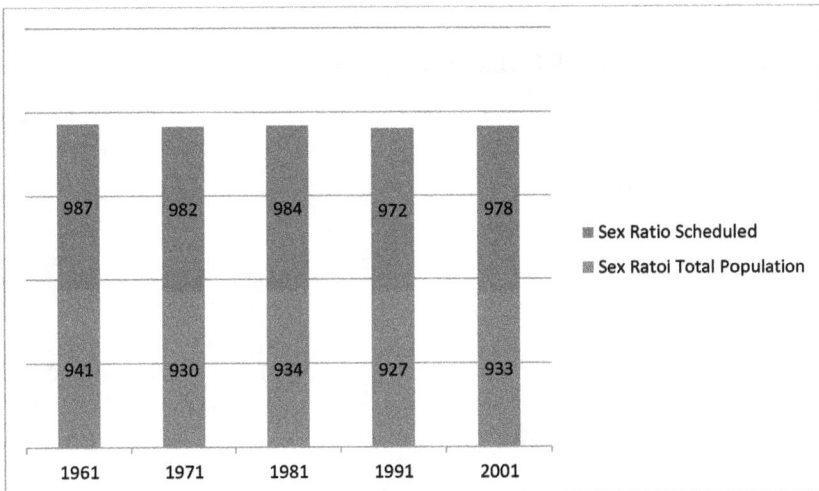

	1961	1971	1981	1991	2001
Sex Ratio Scheduled	987	982	984	972	978
Sex Ratoi Total Population	941	930	934	927	933

Source: Census of India

Changes in Educational Status of Scheduled Tribes

Although, there has been a substantial increase in the literacy rates of scheduled tribes during the last developmental decades, the gap between the literacy rates of STs and those of the general population is not only persisting, but also found to be widening. Adding to this, there are problems of intra and inter-state/district variations in the literacy rates amongst STs. The progress made by STs in comparison to the general population is shown in the Figure IV. As shown in Figure IV, the most discouraging sign was the increasing gap between the literacy rates of Scheduled tribes and of the general categories between 1961 and 2001. While the literacy rate for the general population including STs stood at 64.84 per cent, the same for STs was 47.10 percent in 2001. The decennial growth rate of literacy among Scheduled tribes and general population is shown in the table 10. The literacy of Scheduled Tribes was 8.53 per cent in 1961, which increased to 47.10 per cent in 2001 registering an increase of 38.57 percentages in the last forty years. The literacy rate for the total population in India increased from 28.30 per cent to 64.84 per cent during the period from 1961 to 2001. ST male literacy increased from 13.83 per cent to 59.17 per cent during the period 1961-2001 Female Literacy.

Figure IV: Literacy rate of STs and Total population (1971-2001)   *(In percent)*

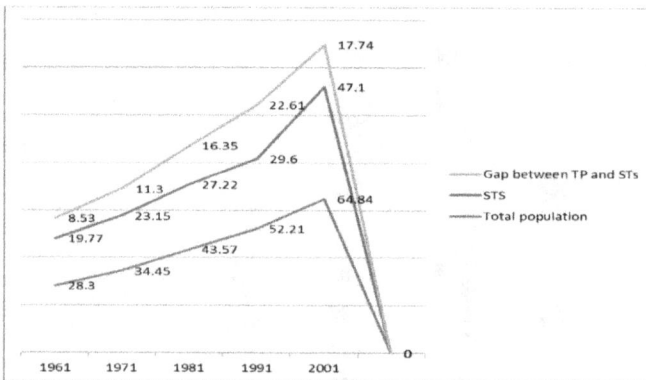

Source: Estimated based on census data

22

Table : 01.06

Decennial growth rate of literacy among Scheduled Tribes and General Category

Year	Schedule Tribe			General		
	Male	Female	Total	Male	Female	Total
1961	13.8	3.16	8.53	40.40	15.35	28.30
1971	17.63	4.85	11.30	45.96	21.97	34.45
1981	24.52	8.04	16.35	56.38	26.76	43.57
1991	40.6	18.19	29.6	64.13	39.29	52.21
2001	59.17	34.76	47.1	75.26	53.67	64.84

Sources: Registrar General of India, Census Operation 2001

Contrary to the efforts of reducing the existing gaps/disparities between STs and the rest of the society, the data in Figure V reveals that although the female literacy rate, which is an important indicator in the field of education, ST female literacy increased from 3.16 per cent to 34.76 per cent during the period 1961-2001, but ST female literacy is lower by approximately 19 per cents point as compared to overall female literacy of the general population in 2001.

Literacy rate of Scheduled Tribes in states of Andhra Pradesh, Arunachal Pradesh, Bihar , Gujarat, J&K, Jharkhand, Karnataka, Madhya Pradesh Orissa, Rajasthan, Tamilnadu, Uttar Pradesh, West Bengal and D&N Haveli is below 50 per cent. As far as STs are concerned, Mizoram had the highest literacy rates in 1991 (82.7%) and 89.3 per cent in 2001. This was the lowest at 19.4 per cent in Rajasthan in 1991 and 28.2 per cent in Bihar in 2001.

Figure V: Female literacy rates of STs and total population   *(In percent)*

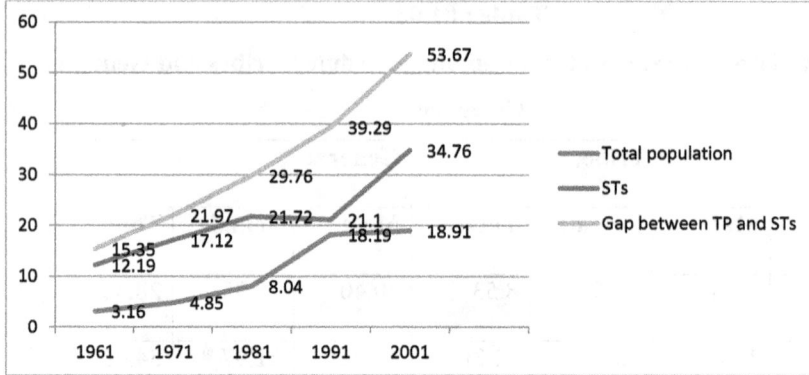

Source: Estimated based on census data

The drop-out rate, which is another crucial indicator in educational development, also shows that there has been a steady decline in respect of both general and STs Categories (Table : 01.07).

Table : 01.07

Dropout rates of Scheduled tribes at various stages of education

Drop-out Rates (%)						
Year	Primary (I-V)		Elementary (I-VIII)		Secondary (I-X)	
	STs	All	STs	All	STs	All
1996-97	56.5	40.2	75.2	56.5	84.2	70.0
1997-98	55.1	39.2	73.0	56.1	75.8	69.3
1998-99	55.7	41.5	72.4	56.3	82.2	66.7
2001-02	52.3	39.0	69.5	54.6	81.2	66.0
2002-03	51.4	34.9	68.7	52.8	80.3	62.6

2003-04	48.9	31.5	70.1	52.3	79.3	62.7
2004-05	42.3	29.0	65.9	50.8	79.0	61.9
Decrease in 2004-05	14.2	11.2	9.3	5.7	5.2	8.1

Source: Selected Educational Statistics, 2004-05, MHRD.

The data on dropout rate for the period 1996-97 to 2004-05 indicates decreasing trend and the decrease in percentage which shows an improvement for STs in all categories of school education. For Primary level (I to V classes), dropout rate for all India decreased from 40.2 percent to 11.2 percent for all children during 1996-97 to 2004-05, against 56.5 percent to 14.2 percent for only Scheduled tribes during the same period. For Elementary level (I to VIII classes), dropout rate for all India was 56.5 percent during 1996-97, which decreased to 5.7 percent by 2004-05 for all children, where as it is 9.3 percent for only Scheduled tribes in the same period. For Secondary education level (I to X classes), dropout rate for all India during 1996-97 to 2004-05 decreased from 70 percent to 8.1 percent for all children, where as it is 5.2 percent for only Scheduled tribes in the same period.

Changes in Health Indicator of Scheduled Tribes

Figure VI: Birth Rate, Death Rate and Infant Mortality Rate of India

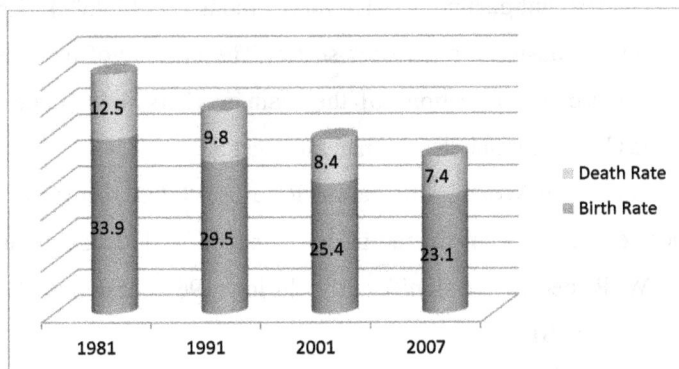

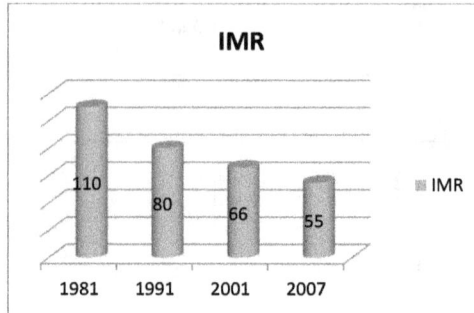

IMR

1981   1991   2001   2007

110   80   66   55

Source: S.R.S Bulletin, October, 2008

The IMR under rate of the country has decreased from 110 to 66 from 1981 to 2001.

Further it reduced to 55 in 2007. Birth rate per 1000 populations was 33.9 in 1981, which reduced to 23.1 in 2007. Similarly death rate was 7.4 in 2009 as against 8.4 in 2001 and 12.5 in 1981.

Changes in Occupation Pattern of Scheduled Tribes

Occupational classification of main workers from 1961 to 2001 among STs and total population is given in the table 12. The data shows that cultivators decreased in both categories over a period of decades from 1961 to 2001. Although, the number of agricultural labourers have increased in all categories, increase has been more among STs. In household industries, the share of all the communities (2.18%) has decreased, but decline is much more among STs (2.46%). Other workers occupations include industry and services sector. The number of other workers has witnessed an increase in all sections of the main workers though the increase in general categories has been much more than amongst ST.

On the other hand Work Participation Rate of ST has increased by 7.8% as against 3.8 per cent to the total for the period 1961 to 2001. It is also important to note that the WPR decreased significantly during 1961-71among all section as reflected in the Figure VII.

Table : 01.08

Occupational classification of main workers (%)

Main workers	Total					ST				
	1961	1971	1981	1991	2001	1961	1971	1981	1991	2001
Cultivators	52.78	43.38	41.53	39.74	31.7	68.18	57.56	54.43	54.50	44.7
Agricultural Labourers	16.71	26.32	25.16	19.66	26.5	19.71	33.04	32.67	32.69	36.9
Household Industry	6.38	3.55	3.99	2.56	4.2	2.47	1.03	1.42	1.05	2.1
Other Workers	24.13	26.75	29.32	38.04	37.6	9.64	8.37	11.48	11.76	16.3

Source: Census of India, 2001

Changes in Poverty Scenario of Scheduled Tribes

The strategy of promoting employment-cum-income generating activities to alleviate poverty amongst STs has proved to be effective in raising a large number of ST families above the Poverty Line during the period between 1993-94 and 2004-2005, as quantified at table 13. Along with the general population, the percentage of ST families living below the poverty line has also shown a declining trend between 1993-94 and 2004-2005.

Table : 01.09

Percentage of People living below Poverty Line (%)

Category	1993-94		1999-2000		2004-05		Percentage Change	
							(Col.2-6)	(Col.3-7)
	Rural	Urban	Rural	Urban	Rural	Urban	Rural	Urban
1	2	3	4	5	6	7	8	9
Total	37.27	32.36	27.11	23.65	28.3	25.7	(-) 8.97	(-) 6.66
STs	51.94	41.14	45.86	34.75	47.3	39.9	(-) 4.64	(-) 1.24
Gaps	14.67	8.78	18.75	11.1	19	14.2	(+) 4.33	(+) 5.42

Source: Planning Commission

However, it is discouraging to note that the rate of decline in respect of STs is much lower than that of the general population. Also, the gap between the poverty rates of the general population and of the STs has increased during the same period. Further, the incidence of poverty amongst STs continues to be very high with 47.3 and 39.9 percent living below the poverty line in rural and urban areas respectively when compared to the figures of 28.3 and 25.7 percent, in respect of total population in 2004-2005. This is primarily because of number of STs are landless with no productive assets and with no access to sustainable employment and minimum wages. The ST women suffer from the added disadvantage of being denied of both equal and minimum wages.

Schemes for the Development of Scheduled Tribes

Efforts made from the beginning of the planned era through various developmental plans, policies, special strategies and programs. The major schemes/programme for the development of scheduled tribes are as follows:

1. Special Central Assistance (SCA) for Tribal Sub-Plan (TSP)

This is a major Programme for the focused development of tribals and tribal areas. Started in the fifth five-year plan, the special central assistance is provided by the government of India to the Tribal Sub-Plan of States/UTs as an additive to the state plan to fill gaps in the budgetary provisions towards TSP. It is basically meant for Family Oriented Income Generation (FOIG) schemes in sectors like agriculture, horticulture, minor irrigation, soil conservation, animal husbandry, forest, education, cooperatives, fisheries, village and small industries etc; and infrastructural development incidental there to. The assistance given is hundred percent and it is expected to act as a catalyst for giving a boost to investment by the State governments and financial institutions. The release of fund is broadly on the basis of the scheduled tribe population, geographical area and inverse proportion of per capita net state domestic product. The State Government in turn releases funds on the basis of certain norms for ITDPs, MADA pockets, clusters, Primitive Tribal Groups and dispersed tribal groups. About 70 percent of the SCA fund is spent on family oriented schemes and only 30 percent on the infrastructure incidental to such schemes. There is a thinking to change this proportion by assigning 80 percent of the SCA funds to infrastructure development and only 20percent for individual/ family oriented schemes since individual/family oriented schemes can be taken up under the schemes of the Ministry of Rural development and also funded through the National Scheduled Tribes Finance and Development Corporation. The Ministry of Tribal Affairs has also found that there is no check or monitoring of the release of SCA funds by the State Governments to the implementing agencies. Moreover there is also unusual delay in the release of SCA funds by the State Governments to the implementing agencies. Some states have also not opened separate budget heads for showing the TSP funds.

The following statement will show that after the introduction of TSP concept in the fifth five-year plan, there has been a tremendous increase in the flow of funds for tribal development.

Table : 01.10

Total Plan outlay for Tribal Development

(Rs. In crores)

Five Year Plan	Total Plan outlay	Tribal Development Programmes/ Flow to TSP	Percentage
First plan	1960	19.93	1.0
Second plan	4672	41.92	0.9
Third plan	8577	50.53	0.6
Fourth plan	15902	75.00	0.5
Fifth plan	39322	1102.00	3.01
Sixth plan	97500	5535.00	5.00
Seventh plan	1,80,000	10,500.00	5.00
Eighth plan	1,66,756.36	15,800.05	9.47
Ninth plan	2,89,147.14	23,375.08	8.08

Source: Annual Report of the Ministry of Tribal Affairs (2008-2009)

2. Grants under Article 275(1) of the Constitution

Every year, funds are released to the State Governments to meet the cost of such schemes of development as may be undertaken by them for promoting the welfare of Scheduled Tribes and for raising the level of administration of the Scheduled Areas to that of the rest of the state. The objective is to promote the welfare of Scheduled Tribes and better administration of Scheduled Areas. The scheme covers all Tribal Sub-Plan and tribal majority states of the country. This is a central sector scheme and 100 percent grants are provided by the Ministry of Tribal Affairs to the State Governments. The grants are provided on the basis of Scheduled Tribe population percentage of the state. The Ministry, which earlier used to release the funds without identifying the projects, has now decided to release funds to the State Governments against specific infrastructure development and welfare projects from 2000-2001.

3. Boys and Girls Hostels for Scheduled Tribe Students

This is a centrally sponsored scheme launched in the year 1961-62 with central assistance limited to 50 percent of funds provided by the State Governments. This is given for construction of hostel building and extension of existing hostels. In the case of Union territories, the Central Government releases 100 percent as assistance. The maintenance of these hostels and their buildings are the responsibility of the State Governments/UTs. This is a useful scheme for enabling the Scheduled Tribe students to study in hospitable environments and promoting literacy among tribal girls and boys who have many hurdles due to poor socio-economic condition.

Since the land for the building is to be provided by the State Governments free of cost and moreover, 50 percent of funds are to be provided by them, there has been poor demand for the construction of the new hostels. The State Government has also to bear the recurring and non-recurring expenditure for running and maintenance of these hostels.

4. Ashram Schools in TSP Areas

This is a centrally sponsored scheme launched during 1990-91 with an objective to extend educational facilities like establishing residential schools for Scheduled Tribes in an environment conducive to learning. The funds under the scheme are given to the states on a matching basis i.e. 50.-50 while100 percent assistance is given to the UTs. The scheme provides funds for the construction of school building from the primary standard to the senior secondary stage of education. It also allows for up-gradation of existing primary level Ashram schools.

Under this scheme, besides the school building, the construction of hostels for students and staff quarters are also undertaken. The State Government has to provide land free of cost for such constructions. Grant is provided for expenditure of other non-recurring items like purchase of furniture, equipments, and sets of books for school and hostel library. A sum of Rs.44.86 crores was earmarked for this Programme in the Ninth five year plan. This scheme suffers from the same ailment namely the failure of the state governments to provide 50 percent fund out of their own budgets.

5. Scheme for Educational Complex in low Literacy Pockets for Development of Female Literacy

It is known that the literacy level among females in the Scheduled Tribes is abysmally low. This scheme is meant to tackle this problem through identification of 134 districts in the country, which have below 10 percent literacy rate among Scheduled Tribe females. The scheme is implemented through NGOs, corporate societies and State Governments.

The primary objective of the scheme is promotion of education among tribal girls in the identified low-literacy districts of the country. The secondary objective is to improve the socio-economic condition of the poor and illiterate tribal population. It is a central sector scheme and the government of India provides 100 percent funds. The educational complexes are established in the rural areas of the notified districts and have classes from I to V with provision for up-gradation up to XII provided they have sufficient accommodation for class rooms, hostels, kitchen, and gardening and for sports. These educational complexes impart not only formal education to tribal girls but also train the students in agriculture, animal husbandry and other vocations and crafts which will make them skilled for ,leading a better life. The teaching from class I to III is done in the tribal dialects of the area and women having proficiency in tribal dialects are engaged as teachers.

Though the strength of students in each class has been fixed at 30, a maximum of 10 more students, if available in the locality, are admitted as day scholars. The

32

recurring grants provided to run the educational complexes is Rs.9000/- per student per year. This includes expenses on accommodation, food, clothing, payment of salary to teachers etc.

The students are provided two sets of uniform, one set of school books besides free food and medicine. Besides the above, the student's parents are given the incentive of Rs. 50/- per month. A sum of Rs.1000 per student is also given as a non-recurring grant for purchase of cots, mattresses, utensils, etc. Under this scheme, 128 Educational complexes have been established from the year 1995- 96 to 2000-01.

6. Scheme for Vocational Training in Tribal Areas

Realizing the need for skill up-gradation and to equip the tribal youths for self employment, this scheme was introduced in 1992-93 and is continuing since then.
The main aim of the scheme is to develop the skill of the tribal youths for a variety of Trades and prepare them for new job opportunities as well as self-employment in area close to their villages as well as outside. The secondary aim is to improve the socio-economic condition of tribal youths by enhancing their earnings.

This scheme covers all the states and union territories and 100 percent grants under the schemes are provided to states/UTs and other organizations implementing the scheme.

These organizations can either be set up by the Government as autonomous bodies under State or Central Government or NGOs registered under the Societies Registration Act, 1960.

7. Scheme for Development of Particularly Vulnerable Tribal Groups (PTGs)

These groups practicing primitive agricultural practices and having low level of literacy and stagnant or diminishing population face various problems in their progress and development. To cater to the need of such group, a separate scheme was introduced in the year 1998-99 which mainly focuses on ensuring food security and the protection and development of PTGs.

The objective and purpose of this scheme is that funds under the central sector scheme for the development of PTGs will be available only for those items/ activities which though very crucial for the survival, protection and development of PTGs are not specifically catered to by any existing scheme. The activities under the scheme may include measures such as awareness generation and confidence building, training for skill development, improvement in agriculture technology, housing, education and health standards.

The scheme covers 75 PTGs spread over 18 states and one UT. 100 percent funds are provided by the Ministry of Tribal Affairs for the programmes mentioned above. Those activities which focus on helping the beneficiaries to cope up with extreme adverse conditions threatening their survival are taken up on priority basis.

8. Educational Development of Scheduled Tribes

For the promotion of education among the Scheduled Tribes, the following schemes are in operation:

(a) Centrally sponsored scheme of post-matric scholarship.

(b) National overseas scholarship scheme for higher studies abroad.

(c) Book bank scheme.

(d) Scheme of up-gradation of merit.

(e) Coaching for competitive examinations.

9. Promotion of Voluntary Efforts

The roles of voluntary Non-Government Organizations become important as many of them have been rendering yeoman services in the tribal communities of the area. For this purpose the Ministry of Tribal Affairs supports many welfare programmes especially in the field of education and medical care run by the NGOs through the scheme of grant-in-aid to the voluntary organizations working for the welfare of Scheduled Tribes. This scheme is in operation since 1953-54 but its scope has been increased from the year 1998-99. The schemes run through NGOs include residential school, hostels, medical centres, and computer training centres, shorthand

34

and typing units, balwadis, libraries and audio-visual units. 90 percent of the fund for a Programme is given by the Ministry and 10 percent is to be contributed by the NGOs. From the year 1999-2000, 100 percent fund is also available to the NGOs working in the Scheduled areas.

The main objective of the scheme is to provide for an over-all improvement and development of the Scheduled Tribes through voluntary efforts in the field of educations, health and sanitation, environment, drinking water, legal redressed service and those need-based socio-economic upliftment efforts having direct beneficial impact on the target groups.

10. Schemes for the Financial Assistance to Scheduled Tribes

A new National Finance and Development Corporation meant for the economic development of Scheduled Tribes has been started in the year 2001 after bifurcation of the National SC and ST Finance and Development Corporation. This Corporation would provide financial assistance at concessional rates for income generating activities and training in skill development to STs whose annual income is below double the poverty line. This assistance for self-employment purposes would be available up to Rs.10 lakhs through the State channelizing agencies which are in many cases the state Scheduled Tribes Finance and Development Corporation. The projects undertaken under this Programme should be technically feasible and financially viable. The Corporation would provide term loan, seed capital, bridge loan etc. at concessional rates of interest. The maximum amount available would be 85 per cent of the project cost with 10 percent coming from the State Corporations and 5 per cent from the beneficiary concerned. It provides finance in the sectors of agriculture, horticulture, animal husbandry and dairy, minor irrigation, small industries, small trade and transport services. This scheme will also help in removing indebtedness among tribal and provide finance at concessional rates which the commercial banks have so far failed to provide.

Due to the backwardness and low socio-economic development among STs, Government has made affirmative policies, Programmes and enacted laws. There are many Constitutional safeguards for the welfare, development and protection of STs in the country besides National Commission, 5th and 6th Schedule for the protection and administrative dispensation of tribals in the Central Indian States and North-Eastern Region States, "The Provision of Panchayats (Extension to the Scheduled Areas) Act, 1996 which confers special powers to Gramsabha in 5th Scheduled Areas, "Forest Rights Bill", "Land Rehabilitation & Resettlement Policy". Though these Constitutional provisions are in place the effective implementation of these in letter and spirit by the State is a great impediment for the welfare and development of the SCs and STs in the country.

In spite of the many affirmative actions, tribals in India face insurmountable problems due to their low socio-economic conditions, poverty, unemployment, displacement, indebtedness, lack of opportunities, accessibility and awareness of the government programmes. Coupled to this, the government and private industrial establishments have initiated mega projects of mining, hydro-electric, industry, business, roads and transport which is leading to the loss of traditional land ownership and livelihood opportunities. This is resulting in large scale migration of rural tribal to urban areas in search of livelihoods either temporarily or on permanent basis which in turn resulting into the disturbances of their traditional sociopsychological family relationship, network of neighbourly relationships and the adoption of new urban culture. Human Migration and in particular tribal migration with its implications is becoming an important socio-economic problem for the policy makers and government to undertake welfare and development activities.

Socio-Economic Profile of Jharkhand State
The state of Jharkhand was carved out of the state of Bihar in 2000. Ranchi is the capital of Jharkhand a state that is more famous for the various political happenings than its developments. The captain of the Indian National Cricket team, Mahendra Singh Dhoni hails from Ranchi, the capital of the state. The state has had many challenges in terms of crime and social issues and the governments here have found it difficult to come to terms with the same. The state is located in the eastern

36

part of the country and has Madhya Pradesh and West Bengal as neighbors apart from Bihar and Orissa.

The Population of Jharkhand according to the 2011 census stands at about 32 million, making it the 13th most populated state in India. The state makes up about 3.5% of the country's population a figure which was about 3% during the last census in 2001. The state is spread over an area of about 79000 sq. km. one of the smaller states in the country in terms of area. The density of population per sq. Km. is about 414, which is above the national average by a good 30 points. The state has a growth rate of about 22% which slightly exceeds the national growth rate of about 17%. The population of the state is rising considerably more due to the lack of education and lack of understanding about family planning. The literacy rate in the state is about 67% a figure that needs instant correction and steps to do so need to be put into effect immediately. The sex ratio in Jharkhand is about 940. The statistics in the Jharkhand Census 2011 reveal facts that can be instrumental in planning for a better development plan for the state. The largest city in the state of Jharkhand is Ranchi while Jamshedpur is the capital city of the Jharkhand. The languages spoken in the Jharkhand state includes Hindi. In total Jharkhand (JK) state comprises 24 districts. The ISOCODE assigned by International Organization for Standardization for Jharkhand state is JK. There are 30 STs in Jharkhand and the major among them are Santhal, Oraon, Munda, Ho, Kharia, Bhumji, Lohra, Kharwar, Chero, Bedia, Mal Paharia and Mahli are the main STs in Jharkhand. The majority of the ST population, about 91.7%., lives in rural and forest areas. Gumla, Purbi Singhbum, Lohardaga, Pashchimi Singhbhum, Dumka, Giridih, Ranchi, Sahibganj, Gumla and Pakur are the main districts with higher concentration of the Scheduled Tribe population.

The sex ratio of the ST population in Jharkhand is 987 females per 1000 males that is higher than the national average of 978 for the same population category. Compare to the literacy rate of 27.50 percent in 1991 it has increased up to 40.70 percent in 2001 among the ST population in the State. It is significantly lower than the average national literacy rate of 47.10 percent for the ST population. The male and female literacy rates are 54% and 27.2% in 2001.

The Work Participation Rate of the ST population in Jharkhand in 1991-2001 is 46.30 percent that is lower by about 3.00 percent than the national average of 49.10 percent. Similarly, the main workers in the State constitute 59.40 percent of the total workers which too is lower than the national average of 68.90 percent for the overall ST population. It is interesting to see that the male WPR shows a decline from 53.40 percent to 51.90 percent while the female WPR for the same period shows an increase from 38.30 percent to 40.60 percent. About 50.00 percent of the ST population in Jharkhand is categorized under the 'cultivators' category which is significantly higher than the national average of 44.70 percent while the other 31.00 percent comes under the 'agricultural labourer' category which is lower than the national average of 36.90 percent. 'Other workers' category constitutes 13.50 percent of the total Scheduled Tribe workers in Jharkhand which is again lower than the national average of 16.30 percent. The workforce percentage involved in household industries (HHI) is 3.00 percent, a bit higher than the national average of 2.10 percent.

Source: Jharkhand Government Website at http://www.jharkhand.nic.in

BROAD SOCIO DEMOGRAPHIC PROFILE

Description	2011	2001
Approximate Population	3.3 Crores	2.69 Crore
Actual Population	32,988,134	26,945,829
Male	16,930,315	13,885,037
Female	16,057,819	13,060,792
Population Growth	22.42%	23.19%
Percantage of total Population	2.72%	2.62%
Sex Ratio	948	941
Child Sex Ratio	948	966
Density/km2	414	338
Density/mi2	1,072	875
Area km2	79,716	79,714
Area mi2	30,779	30,778
Total Child Population (0-6 Age)	5,389,495	4,956,827
Male Population (0-6 Age)	2,767,147	2,522,036
Female Population (0-6 Age)	2,622,348	2,434,791
Literacy	66.41 %	53.56 %
Male Literacy	76.84 %	63.83 %
Female Literacy	52.04 %	38.87 %
Total Literate	18,328,069	11,777,201
Male Literate	10,882,519	7,646,857
Female Literate	7,445,550	4,130,344

Source: Census of India, 2011 http://www.census2011.co.in

Jharkhand Rural Urban Population 2011

Total population of Jharkhand state, around 75.95 percent live in the villages of rural areas. In actual numbers, males and females were 12,776,486 and 12,278,587 respectively. Total population of rural areas of Jharkhand state was 25,055,073. The population growth rate recorded for this decade (2001-2011) was 75.95%. In rural regions of Jharkhand state, female sex ratio per 1000 males was 961 while same for the child (0-6 age) was 957 girls per 1000 boys. In Jharkhand, 4,367,507 children (0-6) live in rural areas. Child population forms 17.43 percent of total rural population.

In rural areas of Jharkhand, literacy rate for males and female stood at 72.86 % and 46.62 %. Average literacy rate in Jharkhand for rural areas was 61.11 percent. Total literates in rural areas were 12,643,078.

Description	Rural	Urban
Population (%)	75.95 %	24.05 %
Total Population	25,055,073	7,933,061
Male Population	12,776,486	4,153,829
Female Population	12,278,587	3,779,232
Population Growth	19.58 %	32.36 %
Sex Ratio	961	910
Child Sex Ratio (0-6)	957	908
Child Population (0-6)	4,367,507	1,021,988
Child Percentage (0-6)	17.43 %	12.88 %
Literates	12,643,078	5,684,991
Average Literacy	61.11 %	82.26 %
Male Literacy	72.86 %	88.44 %
Female Literacy	46.62 %	67.76 %

The Tribes of Jharkhand

The Jharkhand State has a combination of a variety of tribes (32) and occupational artisan castes. The tribes include two linguistic groups; the Mundari linguistic group –including the Santhal, Ho and Munda; and the Dravidian linguistic group – including the Oraon, Chero and Gond. The tribes range from the surviving remnants of almost pure hunter-gatherers among the PTGs (a group) to settled agriculturist tribes like the Santhal, Ho, Munda, Oraon and Gond. Even today the agriculturist tribes still engage in a considerable amount of gathering activity and there remains evidence of collectivist behaviour in economic activities.

Livelihood System in Tribes

The livelihood systems in the area are primarily dependent on combinations of agriculture, forests and labouring. Due to very small holding and the very low productivity of the land most households eke out a living by maintaining a diversified pattern of occupations; no single activity provides sufficient resources to entirely ensure their livelihood. There are, however, a small number of artisan castes and tribal groups who depend on providing services to the community or on small scale processing and marketing. Women's work is critical for the survival of tribal households both in terms of provisioning food and income as well as in the management of resources. Agriculture in the tribal villages/area is predominantly rain fed and mono-cropped. Amongst the PTGs such as Birhors, Pahari Korwa and Sawar women play an important role in (i) food gathering from the forest; (ii) rope making from the bark of trees & sabai grass; (iii) honey collection; (iv) herbal medicinal plant collection, processing & sale; (v) hunting & trapping, (vi) basket making; (vii) shifting cultivation; (viii) labour; and (ix) fishing. Broadly, tribal livelihood system can be classified into three types. First forest dependent upland systems (aprrox. 20%) are usually located in upper catchments areas and comprising most PTG villages/tolas. Second, mixed systems (approx. 65%), which are usually located in the middle, watersheds and these are partially hilly areas, where communities depend less on forest and place added reliance on agriculture. Farming is mainly single crop with some paddy and vegetable cultivation. Food security extends to three to four months. Third lowland systems (approx. 15%) are located in lower watershed. These communities extend into the lower plains and may have relatively little forest access. They tend to be more multiethnic, have smellers but more intensively farmed land holdings and own more cattle. Double cropping is more common, and if there is supplementary irrigation, even a third crop may be grown. There is a greater reliance on paddy, vegetables are cultivated nearly year round and overall food security can

41

extend from five to seven months. Year round access to most communities allows for greater market orientation. Many fields are already bounded as the terrain is generally flatter and there is better system farming has a longer history, which is reflected in greater productivity per hectare. Distant migration may be less prevalent but local wage-earning opportunities are more available.

Women in Jharkhand

Our society is organized around some given parameters and aims, the functionality of which is ensured by a set of systems and institutions. One of the most pervasive and widespread codes of organization that affects all aspects of the social functioning is the gender system. Gender is a socio-culturally determined identity of men and women. It could be understood as the process of acquisition of qualities, attitude, behaviour patterns and roles through socialization by which biological categories of male and female becomes social categories of men and women the gender differentiating ideology is frequently identified only at the level of the gender systems impact on women. Women are central, not marginal to the making of society and to the building of civilization. Women have been part of preserving the past, which has taken the form of the cultural traditions that provides the link between generations, and connects, past and future. This past is kept alive in poems, myths and symbols, which both men and women created and preserved in folklore, art and rituals. For long, what women have done and experienced has been neglected, left unrecorded and ignored in interpretation. Gender is to be seen in totality in understanding and analyzing women's subordination. The term subordination of women is wider in its usage and focuses more specifically in describing the condition of women. Subordination inherently includes the possibility of acceptance of subordinate status in exchange for protection and privilege, a condition, which characterizes so much of the historical experience of women. It shows the dominance of women by men within the society. The impact pertains to the manifestation of gender ideology in women's illiteracy, exploitation and low sex ratio, lack of economic autonomy or physical insecurity.

Communicable Diseases

All the major communicable diseases like tuberculosis, malaria and leprosy are endemic in the state. Tuberculosis contributes maximum to the mortality due to the communicable diseases. Every year nearly 60000 new patients of TB are occurring in the state. The entire state is to be covered under the RNTCP by 2004. Secondly the state has the highest prevalence of leprosy in the country i.e., 14 per 10000 populations in 2000, which has now come down to 4.9 in 2003. Thirdly malaria has been wrecking havoc in the state. In recent years thousands of malaria cases and many confirmed cases of deaths due to malaria were reported. The efforts of the Health Department have reduced the cases. About from maternal mortality early marriage frequency and repeated childbearing and discrimination faced throughout the life cycle results in adverse health outcomes like RTI / STIs, uterine prolapsed, etc. (Anita 2012 P. 117)

Gender inequity is a major human right concern in India. It cuts across all other forms of discrimination and represents an added bias denying women and men the freedom to choose the means for their development and growth. Despite Governments increasing concern and endeavour to promote gender equity the disparities have grown vast and a resulting outcome in the poor socio economic condition of women. In the context of Jharkhand there exists a major difference in the child sex ratio and life expectancy at birth of the state. Social status of Jharkhand women like any other community of India is realized on the traditional patriarchal form which since ages has succeeded in having a control over different areas of women's lives. Their role is exclusively defined in terms of household management and matrimonial duties. They are subjected to expectation that they replenish the race by bearing children. For majority of them, life itself has been a long hurdle race, both within and outside the family. Women in Jharkhand are not very different from women elsewhere in the country in terms of discrimination and disadvantages. There are a number of common characteristics, which the women of Jharkhand share with their counterparts, mainly their level of literacy and education, doing unpaid work, low participation in the work force, very little property rights and even discrimination within the family.

Every society is characterized by the culture of its own, code, social discipline and clear perceptions of dos and don'ts for women segment. Strong tribal culture as well as non-tribal jointly forms the cohesive culture of its own kind in Jharkhand. In case of tribal systems of culture they live in definite geographical areas with their own dialects, culture, art, folk songs, dance and different social norms. Their own traditional business and homogeneous social and economic institutions operate among them as unifying factor. A tribal society is largely isolated from other communities but closely knitted among themselves and organized on the line of kinship, wherefrom the qualities of truthfulness, honesty, duty bound ness and simplicity have developed owing to collective property relationship. But, their culture is vanishing slowly by the impact of modernization. The State is a vast reservoir of natural resources like coal, iron and various other minerals. The proximity to the rich mines has led to the establishment of a number of iron and steel industries in the state. In spite of these moves towards industrialization, the plight of the people in the state does not show a very rosy picture with some of the indicators of Human development Rank lowest among.

The concept of health, of disease of treatment of life and death is as varied as their culture. The usual theory of disease in tribal society is that it is caused by the breach of some taboos by host ill spirits, the ghosts or the dead. Sickness is the routine punishment for every lapse and crime meted out to then by these spirits. As a matter of fact, disease to a tribal mind is like another phenomenon of the natural world, is many faceted and essentially in comprehensible in the sense that no singly theory will cover all the known facts perfectly.

Women's access to health services is much less in comparison to men. The underlying reason being their lower status in the family and lack of decision making power regarding ill health, expenditure on health care and non availability of health care facilities prevent them from seeking medical help. Women wait longer than men to seek medical care for illness. This is partly due to their unwillingness to disrupt household functioning unless they become incapacitated. (Chaudhary. Anita 2012 P. 115)

The availability of health services in terms of infrastructure and personnel is also quite dismal. In all these years, though the government has acknowledged the requirement and presence of certain facility in reality. There exits huge gaps, this to some extent, explains why our health system has not been able to address the huge disease burden, especially in the rural areas (Chaudhary, anita 2012 P. 104).

Tribal Women and Livelihood

Women among the tribal population have very important role in the agriculture-cum-forest-based economies. Women's work is regarded as crucial for the survival of tribal households in terms of provisioning for food, income, earning and management of financial resources. Food gathering is also a vital economic activity even for women of agricultural tribes. Women are major earners from the sale of NWFPs especially in forest dependent livelihood systems. Due to tribal women's role in trade and marketing and to having primary responsibility for household provisioning, they are the de facto managers of most household income, as well as of the agricultural produce. In order to ensure women's productive and effective participation in the development, intensive and sustained training on an on-going basis would have to be given. Women would also be encouraged to go on exposures and training outside the village, as the exposure to areas of new developments on different sectors which would relevant in opening the windows of livelihood opportunities.

Economic Role of Tribal Women

Tribal women in India contribute positively towards economic pursuits by anticipating equally with men folk. They participate in all agricultural operations like sowing seeds, weeding and harvesting, felling and burning trees. In plough based cultivation, transplantation, weeding, winnowing and dehiscing is done entirely by women. They work in all sectors of indigenous cottage industries, tribal arts and production of crafts. Generally, the ploughing is done by men but in some tribal societies, women do the ploughing too. Though the women work for more time than men, they receive less wages and that too in kind which are enchased by males. However, there are some tribes where men and women are equal partners in socio-cultural and economic life and hence women are traditionally assigned an important role in the society (Singh, 1994 : 9; 10).

Low Status of the Tribal Women

The tribal woman does not have property rights except in a matrilineal society which is a small proportion of the tribal population. She is paid less wages than her male counterpart for the same work. Besides this, the women work for more time than men, they receive wages in kind which are enchased by males. The women do not have the decision making power. The division of work is heavily loaded against the tribal woman because in addition to an equal share in the economic production process she has to take the sole responsibility of household chores. In certain tribes only the males can participate in ancestor worship. Usually she cannot hold the office of a priest (Rajya lakshmi, 1996 : 18, 19).

Women have to face several difficulties within and out of the family such as harassment for dowry, rape, molestation, discrimination and denial of their property rights. In addition to these difficulties, there are several other kinds of harassments that women have to suffer. These cruelties are mainly physical. If we look at the national statistics almost 31 women are raped everyday and there is a report of physical molestation after every 15 minutes. These figures relate only to the reported cases. Data related to all the reported cases of violence against women in Jharkhand between the year 2000-2002 is presented below.

Table : 01.11

Atrocities on women in Jharkhand in 2000-2002

S. No.	Year	Rape	Abduction	Dowry Death	Sexual Exploitation	Domestic Violence	Child Abuse	Polygamy	Total
1	2000	553	82	187	213	396	NA	NA	1430
2	2001	578	75	168	239	402	NA	NA	1462
3	2002	679	207	235	190	298	NA	NA	1609

Source: Crime Investigation Department, Jharkhand

Table : 01.12

Atrocities on women in Jharkhand between1998-2002

S. No.	Year	Murder	Dowry Death	Severe Injury	Rape	Eve Teasing	Dowry Cases	Torture	Total
1	1998	36	190	10	466	158	251	421	1532
2	1999	36	149	8	477	146	244	524	1584
3	2000	53	187	8	553	212	272	478	7863
4	2001	65	163	8	578	239	270	477	1805
5	2002	105	235	15	679	190	286	505	2015
	Total	295	929	49	2753	945	1323	2405	8699

Source: Crime Investigation Department, Jharkhand

Both the tables depict an increasing trend of violence against women in the state of Jharkhand.

Table : 01.13

Violence against Women*(1990-1999)

Year	Rape	Dowry Death	Torture
1990	9,518 (13.9)	4,826 (7.1)	13,450 (19.7)
1996	14,846 (12.8)	5,513 (4.8)	35,246 (30.8)
1999	15,468 (14.4)	6699 (4.9)	43,823 (32.3)

*Note: Figure in the parentheses is percentages. * Selected crimes*

Source: Crime in India, 1999, National Crime Record Bureau, M/o HA, GOI

The national figures also show a growing trend in cases of violence against women.

Table : 01.14

Violence against women in districts of Jharkhand

Districts	1999	2000	2001	2002 (May)
Ranchi	66	68	81	21
Gumla	60	51	40	08
Simdega	—	05	23	04
Lohardaga	15	15	17	04
W. Singhbhum	56	45	40	06
Seraikela	—	—	16	07
East Singhbhum	47	53	67	23
Hazaribag	44	54	53	24
Koderma	13	12	04	02
Giridih	66	40	34	17
Chatra	07	10	08	04
Palamu	17	19	20	03
Latehar	—	01	09	02
Garhwa	10	14	15	05
Dhanbad	47	42	44	07
Bokaro	31	39	34	17

Dumka	36	46	34	16
Jamtara	—	03	08	02
Deoghar	29	35	29	10
Godda	13	30	42	12
Sahebganj	15	33	23	05
Pakur	21	19	26	11
Total	**593**	**634**	**667**	**210**

Source: Prabhat Khabar date: 10.01.2003

Rape

Rape is one of the most heinous crimes against women. It has a very deep physical, mental, psychological and social impact on women. Therefore, while looking at violence against women, one has put a special focus on cases of Rape. According to the Indian Penal Code amendment Act 1983,any person committing this crime is liable to 7 years or life imprisonment. If a Govt. servant on duty violates a woman during his duty hours, he can be sent to jail for 10 years or can get life imprisonment.

Table : 01.15

Rape Cases Registered in the Coal Belt

Year	No. of Cases	Accused	Arrested
1997	33	47	28
1998	47	72	55
1999	44	57	54
2000	41	59	55
2001	45	58	55
2002 (Till Aug)	20	12	12

Source: Hindustan Times, Date 04.10.02

The above data depicts a fall in the number of rape cases in the coal belt of Jharkhand.

Many women don't approach police for fear of dishonour or that they will be dismissed or further abused. Many tribals are not aware of their rights under special legislation designed to protect them, and it is rare for police to voluntarily inform them.

Police are also accused of withholding and destroying evidence in many cases, usually at the behest of the accused with whom they may have caste or other links. Witnesses often withdraw their testimony after taking a bribe or being threatened by the accused and medical evidence is lost because simple procedures are not followed. The length of time it takes to pursue a case of torture through the courts encourages victims to make compromises under pressure.

Domestic Violence

In recent years, there has been growing concern about domestic violence in India. NFHS-2 found that in Jharkhand there is widespread acceptance among ever-married women that the beating of wives by husbands is justified under some circumstances. Almost two-fifths (38 percent) of ever married women accept at least one of six reasons as a justification for a husband beating his wife. Domestic violence is also fairly common. Twenty-two percent of even married women in Jharkhand have experienced beatings or physical mistreatment since age 15, and 16 percent experienced such violence in the 12months preceding the survey. Most of these women have been beaten or physically mistreated by their husbands. Domestic violence against women is more prevalent in rural areas, among illiterate women, among women from households with a low standard of living, and among working women.

Table : 01.16

Profile of Domestic Violence in Jharkhand

Age	% of women Beaten	% of women beaten by husband	% of women beaten by relative	% of women beaten by others
15-19	13.5	11.8	2.8	3.7
20-29	21.4	19.7	2.5	1.9
30-39	26.6	25.2	2.4	2.0
40-49	17.6	16.6	1.0	2.7
After 5 yrs. of Marriage	13.6	11.5	2.1	1.4
Betwen 5-8 yrs. of Marriage	19.2	18.6	1.6	1.3
After 10 yrs. of Marriage	24.4	23.1	2.2	2.0

Source: Prabhat Khabar date 2.10.2002

NFHS-II found that in Jharkhand there is a widespread acceptance among ever-married women that the beating of wives by husband is justified under some circumstances. Almost 2/5th (38%) of ever married women accept at least one of the six reasons as justification for a husband beating wife.22% of ever married women in Jharkhand have experienced beating or physical mistreatment. Domestic violence against women is more pronounced notice of Commission in rural areas, among illiterate woman, among women from households with low standard of living (NCW report).

REFERENCES

Bas, Marcel
:An Introduction to Afrikans and the discrimination it faces Downloaded from website www.roepstem.net

Bhowmik, K. L. and Gupta, Samar.
:"Tribal India: a profile in Indian Ethnology", Institute of Social Studies (Calcutta, India). Research Division.

Brysk, Alison
:"From tribal village to global village", Indian rights and International relations in Latin America.

Chaudhuri, Buddhadeb
:"Tribal development in India: problems and protects". Cluckman, Max "Politics, Law and Ritual in Tribal Society".

Cobridge Stuart et al.
: "Jharkhand: Environment, Development, Ethnicity".

Devalle , Susana B. C.
:"Discourses of ethnicity: culture and protest in Jharkhand".

Doshi, Saryu
: "Tribal India : ancestors, gods, and spirits".

Dube,S.C.   (1987)
:"Welfare of the Scheduled Tribes" Encyclopedia of Social Work in India Vol.III, pp. 335-344.

Duyker, Edward
:"Tribal guerrillas: the Santals of West Bengal and the Naxalite movement".

Eder, James F.
:"On the road to tribal extinction : depopulation, deculturation, and adaptive well-being among the Batak of the Phillppines".

Galliou, Patrick and Micheal Jones
:"The Bretons", a book review by Dammy Blackwell 2007. Downloaded from website www.Amazon.com.

Jharkhand Participatory Forest Management" By Ministry of Finance, Tribal Institutions, Panchayat Institutions, Jharkhand Forest Department of Economic Affairs and Minsitry of Finance.

Kelkar, Govind and N., Dev
:"Gender and Tribe : Women, Land and Forests in Jharkhand".

Migration of Ethiopians in Canada downloaded from website www.africa.org

Moser, Rupert R. et al., (1977)
:"Aspects of tribal life in South Asia" Proceedings of an international seminar held in Berne.

Mita Shree Mitra, P.V. Kumar, S. Chakraborty and P. Bharti   (2007)
:Nutritional Status of Kamar tribal children in Chhattisgarh, Indian Journal of Pediatrics, Vol. 74, April 2007.

Oran, Karma.
:"The chance and retention of the tribal art & cultural heritage in Indian subcontinent".

52

Ozkan, Rafat Ali and Polat, Kemal	:"Socio-Cultural Life of Crypsies in Southern Kyrgyzstan, The Social Science Journal Volume 42, Issues-3. 2005, pp. 469-478. Downloaded from website www.sciencedirect.com.
Panda, Chandra Govinda. (2006)	:Development of Tribal Women through Self-help Group. In Rural Development in India, ed by Rao; Narasimha C., New Delhi, Serials, pp. 80-89.
Panigrahi, Nilakantha. (2005)	:Tribal development policies: a critical review with special reference to Orissa. In Development, deprivation and welfare policy ed by Mallik, R.M.; Padhi, S. P. Jaipur: Rawat, 2005, pp. 360-395.
Paul, Sujit et. al.	:"Tribal Agriculture and Modernization"
Population of Garhwa	:Downloaded from website www.jharkhand.nic.in
Prakash, Amit	:"Jharkhand: Politics of Development and Identity".
Raha, K. Manis and Coomar, C. Palash	: "Tribal India: Problem Development Prospect".
Rath Chandra, Govind.	:"Tribal Development in India" The Contemporary Debate
Shah, Parth and M, Vidisha	:"Terracotta Reader : A Market Approach to the Environment".
Singh, K. Amar and Rajyalakashmi, C. (1993)	:"A Study on Status of Tribal Women" in Workshop "Status of Tribal Women in India" organized council for social development, New Delhi 22-23 Dec.) NCW
Singh, Suresh K.	:"The Tribal Situation in India", Indian Institute of Advanced Study.
Snehi, Yogesh	:"Focusing on the Tribal situation" Spectrum June 9, 2002. Downloaded from website tribuneindia.com.
Tripathi, S.N. (2006)	:"Impact of Globalization of Tribals in KBK districts of Orissa. In Rural development for social change ed. By Tripathy. S., New Delhi, Sonali Publishers 2006, pp. 20-30.
Upadhyay, R.	:"Impact of Christianity on the tribes of Jharkhand".
India 2007	Publication division, Ministry of Information and Broadcasting, Government of India.
Kung, B.T; Wilson, G. F. and Lawason, T.L. (1986):	: Alley cropping a stable alternative to Shifting cultivation. International Institute of Tropical Agriculture, Ibadan, Nigeria: P 22.

	NAS (National Academy of Science, U.S.A.) 1979, Tropical Legumes: Resources for the future. US National Academy of Science, Washington, DC.
State of Forest Report. 2003	:Forest Survey of India (Ministry of environment and forest) land and water resource for developing Agroforestry based Farming Systems.
Sinha. B.K.P. & Minaketa	:Changing Socio-economic condition and livelihood of geographically isolated tribal community in kandhamal and KBK districts of Orissa', Report of Planning Commissions, Government of India.
NCW Report	:"A Situational Analysis Of Women And Girls In Jharkhand", National Commission For Women New Delhi
ANNUAL REPORT	Ministry of Tribal Affairs Government of India 2012-13,p.30
Jharkhand 2014	Jharkhand Population Sex Ratio in Jharkhand, Literacy rate data http://www.census2011.co.in
Census of India,	:2001, 1991, 1981, 1971 and 1961. Registrar General of Census, Government of India.
Vidyarthi, L.P. and Rai, B.K., 2000	"The Tribal Culture of India",
Tripathi, S.N. (2006)	:"Impact of Globalization of Tribals in KBK districts of Orissa. In Rural development for social change ed. By Tripathy. S., New Delhi, Sonali Publishers pp. 20-30.
Verma, M.M. (1993)	:'Constitutional Provisions and Welfare. Measures for Scheduled Tribes: Are They Still Relevant?' Indore: Ambedkar Journal of Social Development and Justice, Vol.3 (March).

CHAPTER – II
OVERVIEW OF LITERATURE

A review of concept and previous studies is useful to define precisely the concepts used in the present study, to place the problem in proper perspective and to decide the frame work for analysis. Precise definition of concept would enable both the collection of relevant data and meaningful interpretation of the results of analysis.

Concept

The following concepts and terms used in the present study are given below: The term tribe is derived from the Latin word 'tribes' meaning the 'poor or the masses'. In English language the word 'tribe' appeared in the sixteenth century and denoted a community of persons claiming descent from a common ancestor,

Tribes

Anthropologically; a tribe is a social group, the members of which live in a common dialect and uniform. Social organization possess cultural homogeneity having a common ancestor, political organization and religious pattern. But, it would be very difficult to find many tribal groups in India who possess all these characteristics. Again a number of tribal groups are recognized by the government and they are the scheduled tribes, but since all the tribal and analogous social formation are not considered as scheduled tribes, and when the tribal population is considered the number of actual tribal population must be much more than what is mentioned as scheduled tribe population (Chaudhari, 1992).

Some large tribal communities are distributed in wide region and often profess varied occupation. A few tribal groups are divided into a number of sub-groups which are practically distinct tribal groups. In many cases some distinct tribal groups have identical names.

The term tribal refers to a cultural and historical concept. It is used in terms of folk urban continuum along with different groups are classified given a certain order of material, cultural and stage of technological growth and classified as tribes. According to Oxford dictionary, tribe is a group of people in primitive or barbarous stage of development acknowledging the authority of a chief and usually regarding themselves as having a common ancestor.

General View of Women

The concept of women has been best described in an ancient sanskriti saying, **"Yatra Nari Pujyate"** Women have been given as description of mother goddess and are considered the source of shakti. A woman is mirrored the wealth and prosperity of the society to which she belongs. Her role has been duly recognized by the civilized societies and developed economy. The level of development of a country can be best judged by the status it attributes to women. India is the second largest country in the world in terms of female population, which constitutes about half of the total population. A woman is not only a laughter , wife or mother but she is also a social being .A mother's role is more important, as she has to mould the children into a difficult member of the society. Modern women are highly endowed with intelligence foresight, dignity and thoughtfulness to face difficult situations in their homes. Women are endless source of power. She is formidable force that can change the complexion of growth, rejuvenated the human resource, absorbs the strains of modernization and fight the force of destruction.

Social Status

Social status refers to the position of on individual in family which   is determined by social factors like education, caste and economic factors like employment, income and consumption.

According to Lakshmi memon (1969) the social status of women in any community is largely dependent on the cultural tradition of the community as women's primary responsibility is to her family which is widely accepted all over the world.

Social status is the position occupied by a person, family or kinship group in a social system relative to others. This determines right duties and other behavior including the nature and extends the relationalship with persons of other status.

Social Status has hierarchical distribution in which a few persons occupy the highest position. The simplest theoretical model of social system would be a distribution in which position was determined competitively by the demand for abilities in the society. The status is determined by education, income, possession and other activities in society.

Social status is the position of an individual within social relationship. Social status can be both, high or low. There is an order of social status in society. In the past Brahmins enjoyed greater respect and were considered superior to others castes and community.

The social status of an individual is that particular position in relation with other individuals, by virtue of which he is the recipient of respect and prestige and wields influence and which can be recognized by symbols of prestige accruing to him and his action.

The social status of an elderly person is determined by several factors such as physical health marital status level of education, and position in the society.

The social status of women in society is measured in terms of the level of education health, and the role played by them in the family, community and society.

The social status of tribal women of Jharkhand state in the present study is taken to mean the customary, rituals like attending marriage, religious function, and visiting a relative's house.

Economic status

Poul Chudgari (1992) has pointed out that income/employment of an individual determines his/her economic status, Joachim (1989), related economic status to the nature of occupation done by the Christians of scheduled caste origin, total income ,assets possessed by them and their level of indebtedness i.e. assessing whether they are below poverty status or above it.

Padmavathi (1992), refers the term' economic status' to the income available per head of the household of an individual and the expenses incurred per head on food. This term also refers to the level of saving and borrowing by the individual.

In the Present study, the economic status of the Mudaliar Community widows is meant to include ownership of property, employment, income, expenditure and borrowings.

International Study

In 1975, the seventh special session of the United Nations General Assembly, asked for an approach more effective than that of the international development strategy, adopted in 1970 for achieving social distribution and social objective development. The conference on Employment, Income Distribution and social progress organized by the ILO in June 1976 ordered the 'Basic Needs approach' for social development which focuses the achievement of a certain specific minimum standard of living (ILO, 1976). Development, here, was defined as an Endeavour to provide the basic needs of the people. This approach specified that basic needs of the people included not only certain minimum requirements of a family for [riveted consumption such as adequate food, shelter and clothing, but also minimum levels of essential services provided by the government. The approach of poverty alleviation emphasizes that delivery of a basket of "basic needs of the target groups" (Fei and Ranis, 1973; 345).

In 1990 UNDP published the Human Development report. The report defined Human Development as a process of enlarging peoples' choices (UNDP: 1995:46).Obtaining income is certainly one of the main means of expanding choice and well being. But too often the expansion of income is confused with the enhancement of human capabilities.

Human Development reports also define the relationship between human development and economic growth. It centered the conventional wisdom by asserting that there is no atomic link between the two economic growth is essential for human development but specific policy measures are needed to translate economic progress into human progress,

Other theory was presented by (Rostow, 1960), In 1950s distinction between 'growth and development' was not generally accepted by economists. Rather they concaved economic growth as the supreme goal in itself. It was economic growth that they were natural foci for theory formation. The works of W.A. Lewis. Paul Baran, W. Rostow bear ample testimonies in this regard. W.A. Lewis emphasized that " our subject matter is growth not distribution" W.A. Lewis1955 Paul Baran for the most influential development economist among the leftists wrote in 1957, ' on political Economy of growth' and defined "Growth of development as the increase on the per capita production of material goods" (Baran, 1957). Walter Rostow, presented his 'non communist manifesto' in 1960 as a description of the "stage of economic growth assuming that this single variable can characterized a whole society" (Rostow, 1960)

President Truman of USA also emphasized economic aspects of development and said, "We must embark on a bold new programme for making the benefit of our scientific advance and industrial progress available for the improvement and growth of under developed areas." In continuation to this American policy towards Europe put emphasis on economic reconstruction after the destruction of the Second World War. The best Element in this policy was to so called "Marshall Plan: through which loans and massive transfers of resources to Europe was proposed (Leys, 1996).

Tribal Studies in India

The Indian tribal society is a unique society with diversity of nature and people. In our country, known for the extreme poverty of the masses, the tribals constitute the core of the poor. Poverty, poor health and insanitation, illiteracy and other social problems among the tribals are exerting a dragging effect on the Indian economy. The Five Year Plans formulated for implementation of a series of investment-backed schemes and projects for enhancing the socio-economic conditions of the tribals living in the rural and urban areas. Many of the tribes with their forest-dwelling culture do not have the motivation or the skill of settled cultivation. As a result, their land has been alienated to their better endowed tribal neighbours or non-tribals. There have been many tribal studies in India based on tribal economy, land alienation, socio-economic development, tribal culture etc. It is highly imperative to have a look at these tribal studies by various Anthropologists, Research scholars, etc.

A new trend in ethno methodology which came up during the British period was a theory propounded by Vemer Elwin (1943) 'who suggested that tribals should be kept isolated in their hills and forests. Elwin's theory is known in social anthropology as 'public park theory'. He suggested that ordinarily the non-tribal people should not be allowed to enter into tribal pockets without permission of the state government. This system would guarantee the isolation of the tribals.

G.S. Ghurye (1943) contested the theory of public park. He argued that the tribal's were nothing more than backward caste Hindus. They should be treated at par with the Hindus.

Following Ghurye's argument, D.N. Majumdar (1944) took a slightly different position. His suggestion was that the cultural identity of the tribals as far as possible should be retained. He feared that if the isolation was broken the tribals would lose their ethnic identity. To maintain it, he hypothesized that there should be 'selected integration' of the tribals. While spelling out, he argued that not all the elements of civilization should be allowed to enter the tribal areas.

Only those which have relevance with tribal life should be permitted into such areas. Such a policy would keep the tribals away from the vices of urban life.

The scientific study of tribal economy in India was first undertaken by two scholars D.D.N ag and R.P. Saxena. Nag (1958) made an extensive field tour in the areas of Madhya Pradesh like, Mandla, Bilaspur, Durg, Balaghat and studied the Baiga economy in context of general economic theories lying emphasis on the sources of economy of Baigas. Saxena followed a model of Nag and studied the tribals of Western Hills in Madhya Pradesh and presented the economy of five tribes.

These two studies have some limitations like, exclusion of socio-cultural conditions of the tribes on their study areas.

Verma (1959- 1960)' has discussed the socio-cultural organisations of the Sanria paharias, Mal- paharias and Knmarbhag. He has examined various phases of the tribal life, pregnancy and birth, puberty, widow remarriage, place of women in the society, religion, village council and institutions.

N.N. Vyas (1967) presents the historical, social and economic life of the Baniyas ofRajasthan, Andhra Pradesh, Punjab and Gujarat. Yyas thus points out the differences in customs and practices of the Baniyas of different States. This study has a good comparative background; still it has a limitation like unsuitability of the methodology.

Vimal Shah (1969)' studied the tribal economy of Gujarat, based on the All India Rural Development and Investment Survey of the RBI (1961-62) and the study undertaken by the Gujarat State. Shah selected a sample of 1 120 rural households identified from 28 villages. This study has very effectively brought out the tribal economy in Gujarat. He points out that there is very little diversification in occupation. Agriculture continues to be the main stay of tribal population, very little investment is made to modernise it, very few inputs are made to increase the productivity of land, and many people mostly depend upon traditional agencies for their credit requirements. All these are obviously, the characteristics of a subsistence economy.

L.P. Vidyarthi (1970); attempted to examine the impact of urbanisation on tribal culture. He studied the impact of the emergence of a heavy engineering complex in a tribal belt of Chotanagpur, and by analysing the pattern of socio-economic changes that occurred in this region owing to large scale industrialisation.

Speaking about the process of modernisation among the tribal people in India's borders, Roy Burman (1973),' rightly maintains that, tribals live among the non-tribals, but hardly share a common life. Their contacts are few and formal. In fact, according to him, the tribal in urban areas are in neither of the two worlds fully. Many of them adopt the technology, skill of the modern world, still retaining the emotions of the tribal world. At the primitive level of aspiration, tribals were not concerned with the fact that they were a minority at the regional level. Now, with political and occupational aspirations at the regional level and national level, tribals begin to feel themselves as a significant minority. This is the gift of modern education in particular and modernisation in general. Through his study expresses his dissatisfaction regarding the strategies for tribals modernisation.

Dean Joros (1973), in his study, presents his views on the relation between political socialisation of the tribals and integration process or the effect of tribal welfare programmes for their political socialisation. He reveals that by analysing the political socialisation process of tribals, a more complete evaluation of tribal welfare programmes would be ensured. This view is also explained by P.R.G. Mathur (1977). He points out that induction into political culture and integration into the mainstream of national life are part of one and the same process and without political socialisation being achieved, tribals integration into the national social life is impossible. Political socialisation must precede their integration into national life. Motivation and objective underlying the tribal welfare programmes and political socialisation are common.

Nirmal Kumar Bose (1 977), 12 gives some insight into the tribes social life. "Tribes differ from others in their social system. They have retained their own marriage regulation. Almost all marry within their restricted local group, and are sometimes guided by their own elders or political chief in internal and external affairs. In other words, they form socially distinct communities who have been designated as tribes and listed in the Schedule for special treatment, so that within a relatively short time they can come within the mainstream of political and economic life of India".

S.L. Doshi (1978)" takes a case study of Bhils, on the process of unification and integration. He said that, a sort of integration is achieved by the tribals' with the wider society as a result of political unification. They are aware of the working of democracy, democratic institutions and identification with the level of values. This study has limitation like neglecting the economic aspects of tribals.

Gopala Rao. N. (1978)14 examines the process of transfer of land from the tribals to the non-tribals and the various factors influencing such transfers, by taking a case study of Mondemkhal, a mixed village of tribes and castes, at Parvathipwarn taluk of former Srikakulam district. Data were collected by canvassing schedule and by holding prolonged interviews with the tribal elders and village officials. Land has been alienated by some people to finance agricultural operations. Cultivators require cash to buy cattle and to pay the labourers. It is clear from the study, that credit being taken on pledging land led to land alienation. Land has a tremendous prestige value in the rural context and it could stand as a security both for borrowing and lending.

Roy Burman (1978)' speaking about the tribal integration process, points out that, present context integration means four things: independent thinking, democratic style of life, secularism and planned economy. These are urgently needed for the tribals to integrate themselves into the mainstream.

R.S. Sharma (1980)16 has discussed the status of tribals in India during ancient times. The epistemological theoretical perspective about the tribals of this period is very clear. It was the time when the Aryans and, later, the high caste Hindus make all efforts to have their hegemony over the tribals.

Sharma has applied material approach to the study of history. This study of tribals is based on the assumption that the mode of production involving the theory of surplus leading to class formation continues to the best working hypothesis.

Pradeep Kumar Bose (1981),"in his paper, questions the validity of observing stratification pattern among Indian tribes on the basis - of caste hierarchy or 'Sacred' hierarchy or division on class basis. This is observed in the context of Gujarat tribes. Tribal population in modem market and production systems and their incorporation into modern political systems are shown regional variations in occupations, use of modem machinery etc. Data were collected from seven districts of Gujarat, through survey method and random sampling, identifying four distinct classes: rich peasant, middle peasant, poor peasant and agricultural labourers.

Renuka Pameche (1985) has studied political aspects of the Bhils and the process of the formation of elite in Bhil Society - Elaborate accounts of the traditional political system of Bhils and the impact of the modem system on them are given. A serious limitation of this book is that, it has not taken into consideration the socio-economic aspects of the poor tribals.

Alok Kumar (1986) has attempted to analyse and interpret the, socio cultural organisation and economic structure of Mal-paharias tribe of Santalparganas district westwhile Bihar in the light of regional geographical complex. Based on his extensive field work, he examines the land use, income expenditure pattern, size of the families and its geographical ratification. This book provides innate glimpse on the habit of Mal-paharias in regard to their dress, religious ceremonies, customs, hunting, agricultural instruments and musical instruments.

Finally the author observed the major requirements of their settlements and has opined that paying adequate attention to the facilities lacking in their settlements can hasten emerging of Mal-paharias in the mainstream of Indian life. This book will be helpful to scholars and researchers of Geography, anthropology and planners of regional development.

Devendra Thakur (1986) made an elaborate study about the Santhals in eastwhile Bihar. The study highlights their socio-economic conditions. It has been observed to what extent they were responsive to the projects and programmes undertaken during the different development plans.

Before the introduction of Five Year Plans, during the colonial rule, the tribals in the country as a whole remained in isolation. If the problem of untouchables in pre-independent India was that of pollution, vis-a-vis purity, the problem of tribals or adivasis was that of isolation. They were considered backward and savage. Lamenting on such an approach to the study of Indian tribals, Yogendra Singh (1986) observes: The colonial ethnographers, for instance, took a placid, even a synchronic view of the tribal society. The conventional framework development by the British administrators-turned ethnographers and by anthropologists was inspired by the then prevailing model in anthropology. Tribal communities were treated as and the primitive condition was described as a state of Arcadian simplicity. Geetha Menon (1987), reveals that the impact and the loss of common property resources is severe on tribal women. She shows that the hardship of the tribal women have been increasing. Thus tribal women are the major victims of the deprival of the traditional rights of the tribals in common property resources.

Christoph Von Furer - Harnendart (1988), has discussed the pattern and causes of disintegration of the traditional tribal system, failure of welfare programmes by taking the example of two tribes, Apa Tanis of Arunachal Pradesh and Gonds of Andhra Pradesh. He found that the two tribes stood at opposite ends of a spectrum today. While Apa Tanis were clearly set on upward path, the Gonds were threatened by an apparently irreversible decline in their fortunes. He claims that Apa-Tani tribe of Arunachal Pradesh numbered about 15000, achieved development and integration without losing its identity because of protection assured by the Government of India.

Rarnakant Prasad (1988), 26 deals about the tribe of Bihar which has little population and living in different ecological settings. This tribe represents variations within a culture due to various ecological settings. It depicts the total way of the tribe name 'pabhaiya'. This book further illustrates how a small tribe exists with its socio-ecological conditions and the problems they are facing today. It deals with the problems and prospects of the tribe and gives an outline for development and protection of such a marginal tribe in Indian sub-continent.

L.C. Mohanthy (1989), 'has remind us of the urgent necessity of evaluating how far tribals have improved their economic-conditions and how far they have been integrated into the larger Indian society. He believes that giving tribals full freedom to manifest their genius will help their integration.

S.L. Doshi (1990) who has conducted researches on the Bhils of south Rajasthan, argues that in ancient India the tribals did not constitute the core of society. They were always marginalised. Though there are no accounts of their collective identity, it is stated that they practised a pastoral life characterized by animism. They were, by and large, a classless, stateless society tribals.

Madhusudan Trivedi (1991)" presents his views regarding the entrepreneurship among the tribals. He has taken the case study of Bhils in Rajasthan. According to him entrepreneurship is an unorthodox venture for the tribals. In the wake of development they have to take new crops, commercialisation and mechanisation in their agricultural practices. The economic transformation which the tribals witnessed today led them to a capitalist economy. Capitalism has created class stratification among the tribals.

This book focuses on the emergence of capitalism among the tribals and its social consequences on class formation.

Buddudeb Chaudhaudi's (ed.) (1992)" 'Tribal Transformation in India', in five volumes, is a collaborative effort of Indian scholars to capture the changing tribal scenario and a whole diversity of issues related to tribal economy, agronomy, politics, ethnicity, ecology, education, technology transfer, social political movements, religious faiths and rituals in an indigenized, yet more articulate framework, with both diagnostic and remedial models. With the latest concepts of research tools in anthropology and related disciplines, the authors make a fresh look at micro and macro level dynamics of the tribals situation in India. vis-a-vis the socio-cultural relations.

S.G. Deogaonkar (1994) traces the origin and growth of the efforts for the development of tribal population in India. Apart from examining various approaches to tribal development, it enumerates the administrative structures and organisational strategies adopted during the last many years of planning, the outlay on tribals development during the plans and the priorities adopted have also been indicated. The Tribal Sub-Plan strategy and its implementation has been examined elaborately. The personal policy adopted in tribals development finds a special and critical treatment.

Rudolfe Heredia (1995), reveals his view that "if the developmental dilemma that confronts our tribals is to be successfully addressed, tribal integration will require their mobilization not just to preserve their cultural autonomy but to redress their minority status as well" so that they can participate in their own development. For this, tribal education will have to play a major role.

P. Sudhakara Reddy (1995)34 in his comprehensive study, discusses the processes and problems of displacement, rehabilitation and socio-cultural changes occurred among the displaced Scheduled Tribe, Yanadis of the Shriharikota Island in Andhra Pradesh where the rocket launching station was established by Indian Space Research Organisation, government of India. The author also tries to portray the traditional social and cultural fabric and adaptation of the Yanadi islanders prior to their displacement, which serves as the basis for understanding the continuity and change in the environment, society and culture.

He analyses the rehabilitation programmes and the resultant factors and the forces behind the system of forced migration and adaptation of the Yanadis to the new environment, outside the rehabilitation centres. He also describes the pattern and processes of continuity and change on the socio-cultural set up of Yanadi islanders.

Bhujendra Nath Panda (1996), "has made sincere attempt to study the personality adjustment, mental health, attitude and academic achievements of more cultured Saora tribes. Through an in-depth analysis, this book provides practical suggestions to teachers, and policy makers to realise the pros and corns of tribals acculturization. Thus the findings have obvious implication for policy makers in tribal education and development.

S.N. Tripathy's (1999) book contains eleven selected contributions of eminent authors relating to various issues and problems of tribals along with policy options. The role of financial institutions and co-operatives in mitigating the tribals economic problems, the impact of development plans and poverty amelioration schemes, etc., have discussed at length. Based on secondary as well as field data collected through survey, this work portrays the evaluation and analysis of tribals problems and policy paradigms to tackle the problem of backwardness in tribal regions.

P.C. Jain (1999) 'gives some insight into the Bhils and Minas of Rajasthan. The objective of the study is to find out the development attained by these two tribal groups. The development is through various sources. In the First Year Plan, the State government is committed on constitutional ground to bring the tribals at par with the other tribal groups who are economically and socially advanced.

S.R. Bakshi and Kiran Bala (2000) present the socio-economic status of several scheduled tribes inhabiting in various regions of our sub-continent. Their lifestyle, customs and traditions are quite different from the population of our rural and urban areas. In fact 'they live in their own world'. Their social backwardness has been assessed at various levels and schemes have been launched for the education of their children, to provide them health facilities and jobs for their daily needs.

Prakash Chandra Mehta (2000) presents an overall review of the tribal development measures adopted during the 20th century. According to him the government failed to provide them basic minimum needs for their subsistence. The first half of the century was administered by the British government and the local rulers. They were not bothered about the tribals needs and welfare. Hence, during the first half of century they were exploited by the previous rulers.

A Study has been organized by Tirpude College of social work civil line, sadar. On "A migrant tribal women and girls in ten cities: A study of their socio-cultural and economical status and conflict with special reference to social intervention. The study was conducted in thousand of tribal women and girls migrated from their hinterland in the tribal area to urban city centre mainly in search of employment. They are new for the city life style and environment and find it difficult to make adjustment with the changed situation and environment. They have to face number of problem in the cities. They get migrated. Moreover, they are exploited both financially and sexually by the non-tribal in the cities. With a view to examine the socio-economic conditions of these migrant tribal women and girls in the cities and to study the problems faced by them it was proposed to conduct a research study.

Other study has been organized by the Y.G joshi on socio-economic transformation in tribal areas. A telescopic study in western tribal belt of Madhya Pradesh.

The present paper is based on a research project undertaken by the author in collaboration with Dr. Sandeep Joshi at Madhya Pradesh Institute of social Sciences, Ujjain, sponsored by the sponsored by the year 2003. The study pertain to the tribal domination in jhabua district of western Madhya Pradesh. Social change and development are complex phenomena, involving a much wider range of physical, location, economic, socio-political technological and behavioural variable.

Dr. M Shakeel Ahmed discussed in his book named Five decades of planning and tribal development a study of Uttarakhand and Jharkhand. The study has been organized in two states. It is a comparative study of the position of tribal in Jharkhand and Uttarakhand. The field study was first conducted in four blocks of Deharadun district in Uttarakhand namely Chakrata, Kalsi, Daiwala, Vikasnagar in June-July 2003.

REFERENCES

Verrier, Elwin,	(1943)	:'The Aborginals', Oxford University Press, New Delhi.
Ghurye, G.S.,	(1943)	:'The Tribal's so called and their Future', Gokale Institute of Politics and Economics, Poona.
Majumdar, D.N.,	(1944)	:'Races and Cultures of India', Asia Publishing House Delhi.
Nag, D.D.	(1958)	:'Baiga Economy of Madhya Pradesh', M.K. Publications, Calcutta.
Verma, P.,	(1960)	: Socio-Cultural Organisations of Tn'bals, Metro Publishers, Rajasthan.
Yyas, N.N.	(1967)	:'Customs and Traditions of Some Indian Tribes', Vikas Publishing House, New Delhi.
Vimal Shah,	(1969)	:'Tribal Economy in Gujarat, Well Print Publications', Jaipur.
Vidyarthi, L.P	(1970)	:'Socio-cultural Implication of Industrialisation in India', Planning Commission, New Delhi.
Roy Burman, B.K.	(1973)	:'Modernisation of Tribal people on India's Borders', K.S. Mathur, (ed.), Studies in Social Change, Ethnographic and Folk Culture Society, U.P.
Joros, Dean	(1973)	:'Socialisation of Politics', Higgim Bofhem, Madras.
Mathur, P.R.G	(1977)	:'Accountration and integration in Tribal Lge', Inter India Publishers, New Delhi.
Bose Nirmal Kumar,	(1977)	:'Tribal Life in India, National Book Trust', New Delhi.
Doshi, S.L.	(1978)	:'Process of Tribal Unification and Integration', Concept Publishing Company, New Delhi.
Gopala Rao. N,	(1978)	:'Land Alienation - A Menance of Tribal Economy', Tribe, Vol. x, No. 4.
Roy Burman, B.K.	(1979)	:'Some Dimensions of Transformation of Tribal Studies in India', Journal of Social Research, Vol. xxiii, No.3.
Sharma, R.S.,	(1980)	:'Indian Feudalism', MacMillan India Ltd., Delhi.
Pradeep Kumar Bose,	(1981)	:'Stratification among the Indian Tribes', Kuruhhethra.
Renuka Pameche,	(1984)	:'Elite in Indian Society, Print Well Publishers, Jaipur.
Alock Kumar,	(1986)	:'Tribal Culture and Economy', Inter India Publications, Delhi.
Devendra Thakur,	(1986)	:'Socio-Economic Development of Tribes in India', Deep and Deep Publishers, New Delhi.
Singh, Yogendra	(1986)	:'Indian Sociology', Vistar Publication, New Delhi.

Geetha Menon,   (1987) :'Tribal Women : Victims of Development Process', Social Action, October.

S. Ramamani,   (1988) :'Tribal Economy Problems and Prospects', Chough Publications, Allahabad.

Ramakant, Prasad,   (1988) :'A Case Study of Cultural Ecology and Tribal Dynamics', J. K Publishers, Andhra Pradesh.

Mohanthy, L.C.   (1989) :'An Analysis of the improved Economic Life of Tribal's of Orissa and the way towards Integration', Deep and Deep Publishers.

Doshi, S.L.,   (1990) :'Tribal Ethnicity and Class Integration', Rawat Publications, New Delhi, Jaipur.

Trivedi, Madhusudan (1991) :'Entrepreneurship anlong Tribal', Print Well, Jaipur.

Buddudeb Chaudhaudi (ed) :'Tribal Transformation in India', Vol. V, Inter India Publications, New Delhi, 1990

Deogaonkar S.G.,   (1994) :'Tribal Administration and Development', Concept Publishing Company, New Delhi.

Rudolfe Heredia,   (1995) :'Tribal Education need for Literative Pedagogy of Social Transformations', Economic and Political Weekly.

P. Sudhakara Reddy, (1995) :'Displace Population and Social Change', Deep and Deep Publications, New Delhi.

Bhujendra N. Panda, (1996) :'Tribal Education', A.P.H. Publishing Corporation, Delhi.

Tripathy S.N.,   (1999) :'Tribal's in Transitions', Discovery Publishing House, New Delhi.

P.C. Jain,   (1999) :'Planned Development Among Tribal', Prem Rawat for Rawat Publications, New Delhi.

Bakshi S.R., and Kiran Bala, :'Social and Economic Development of Scheduled Tribes, Deep and Deep Publications Pvt. Ltd., Delhi, 2000.

CHAPTER – III
OBJECTIVES AND STUDY DESIGN

After independence, however, the progress of women and of the society years to have been retarded even after forty years, example galore where on the one hand the sensitivity over women's issues is lacking and on the other hand atrocities against women are rising. The all five years plan in India gave a special place to women ranging from welfare to development and now from the development to empowerment. Empowerment and information go hand in hand. Without information no development can have firm roots. Women related issues have many dimensions but they can be summarized as health problems, education related problem, violence, denial and deprivation of home property etc.

Particularly, for household affair, women shoulder all responsibilities. They prepare household budget and keep the daily account. Besides, they go to market and purchase necessary materials either for consumptions or other purpose. In this respect male members depend on females. Majority of rural women are illiterate and live in remote and inaccessible areas where flow of information is intermittent or little. They don't have mobility or access to outside world. They hardly get any trainers to train them in any skill. Women are part of the society and their problems should be treated as society's problems. Thus, it is in the men's interest that efforts should be made to improve women's social, political and economical empowerment.

Origin of the Research Problem

People often talk about upliftment of society. To limit this discussion to a small state like Jharkhand, we find the condition of the tribal quit pitiable. Every year most of the Jharkhand tribals under same pretext or the other leave their villages for metropolitan cities like Delhi and Kolkota. If we strike at the root of the problem we discover that simple women both tribal and non-tribal in Jharkhand state are faced with problems in every aspects. In interior villages' women are boldly declared "dayan" which. They are beaten black and blue. Their land is captured by the big bosses and they are kept starved in the villages or are compelled to go away by the brokers. Findings no anchor in the village, they are brought to the capital cities like Delhi and Kolkota Many girls in Pakur district of Jharkhand are missing but the government does not seem very serious about this issue. Similar is the case of Palamu, one of the backward districts of India. Greed and gain play vital roles in the life of young tribal women. The availability of doctors is not here. Tribal people don't trust on the medical treatment. They prefer their own treatment. Women deliver the babies at home without the help of any trained Dais. They are not aware of their heath. So here women are suffering from various RTI/STI and reproductive health problems. Govt. schemes are there, but tribal people don't trust on them. According to the main findings of the NFHS-2 survey for state of Jharkhand, the literacy rate of Jharkhand is 67.9 per cent of males, 39.4 per cent of females, and 54.1 present for the total population.

According to NFHS-2, only 14 percent female, of births in Jharkhand are delivered at home. Utilization of health services in Jharkhand during pregnancy, during delivery, and after childbirth remains very low. They also point to the important role of traditional birth attendant for the large majority of births that occur at home.

Based on a weight- for-height index (the body mass index), two out of five women in Jharkhand 41% are undernourished. Nutritional deficiency is somewhat more serious for working women. Anemia is a serious problem among every population group in Jharkhand, with prevalence rates ranging from 56to 86% pregnant women suffer from severely anemia.

Jharkhand has experiences of beatings or physical mistreatment since the age of 15, and 16% experienced such violence in the 12 months preceding the survey. Most of these women have been beaten or physically mistreated by their husband. Domestic violence against women is more prevalent in rural areas, among illiterate women, among women from households with a low standard of living and among working women.

Viewing the horrible situation the social worker and the journalist by doing something solid can take such tribal of the dark ditches and directly lanes. The government must frame a clear cut programme for uneducated backward tribal. The constitution talks about equal opportunity. It is a good thing but how to make it reality depends on the cooperation received from all sections of society. It is the need of the hour to study in detail the various problems of the tribal living in the state of Jharkhand.

Tribal women is victimized not only by outsiders, she is also victimized by insiders. In their own society the women bear the heaviest burden. Earlier we have mentioned that it is they who manage the house and manage the families. Men often indulge in gossips and liquor. Normally their work is over when sowing is done. The rest of the agricultural operations are looked often by women. And then, do not have their say in matters of decision (Banu Zenab: 2001, Zool p 141)

Statement of the Problem:

Problems differ from age to age and place in accordance with the changing circumstances. Another important thing about the problems is no problem stands isolated and unrelated to some other problems and that problems breed another problems. But the solutions to the innumerable problems are not easy and quickly found out.

- On the one hand Tribal women are advised by terrorists (Naxalies) to join their camps and take revenge on the affluent class, and on the other hand hidden brokers purchase and push them into the dark lanes of the big cities. In that way the helpless tribal girls are trapped in the net of the brokers. The brokers handle their problems the way they like. Draught or no-drought, they do not get easy earning in their villages. They are illiterate and are employed for working under Mahatma Gandhi National Rural Employment Guarantee Act,

2005 (MNREGA). Here the helpers exploit the situation up to their satisfaction. In short their condition becomes pitiable when they don't get food and fodder for their animals. They turn to small towns and big cities. MNREGA scheme in Jharkhand has been in heated controversy. Lack of education among tribals in villages coupled with helpers of bribery make the situation horrible. Two meals a day become difficult for them. Sometimes they are marked present while actually they remained absent. They don't get work of the prescribed quote and timely payment. So illiteracy is a big problem. Most of them have lands of their own, but not fertile. Sheep and other cattle rearing is one of the main occupations of tribals. Tribal' women are illiterate, superstitious and live in poverty. These women have very little social contacts and they are they depend much upon their occupation. Keeping in view of above mentioned studies and overview of literature a research study was conducted entitled A Study of Socio-economic status of Tribes in Jharkhand State with special reference to women.

Questions answered to be in Study

1. The socio- economic cause responsible for the slow growth of tribal women, with reference to availability of opportunity to tribal society.

2. The Tribal women faced problem of health related. Health is the major component which is related to socio-economic aspects.

3. Tribal women face exploitation at every stage in her life from birth till death.

4. Tribal women from Garhwa district are basically illiterate, and their own traditional culture affect their social, economic needs.

Significance of the Study:

1. Several sociologists and social researchers are engaged in search of problems of the tribal regions today. Every tribal community and region differs each other in their interval structure and environment settings. Obviously, the problem is also

rooted in separate circumstances. However, the basis of these problems are similar.

2. The present study as stated earlier is also a research endeavour which attempts provide the knowledge of Socio-economic status of tribal women. This study is empirical in nature and therefore the tools and procedure needed for scientific social research have been followed and applied to collect the information.

3. The proposed study shows significant impact on the existing schemes for Tribal Development to take more and more effective steps in terms of basic needs, livelihood options, and access to knowledge for tribe. Proposed study is an instrument of development to achieve goals of economic growth, social development, environmental sustainability etc. The lack of infrastructure such as lack of adequate schools or health centers, drinking water, sanitation and hygiene facilities affects social life of tribals. These are the major reason why tribal women continue to face problems such as poor literacy rates, or health issues. Specific suggestions are needed to strengthen the policies and plans meant for tribes. The proposed study is an attempt to understand the problems of Tribal women in a wide perspective. All issues related to women, adolescents boys and girls and children will be focused in the proposed study. Keeping in view all aspects of tribal women's problems the proposed study is to go in to the deep root causes of the problems.

4. Thus, this study may help to understand the major problems of tribal women in Garhwa district as a whole. This study also attempts to understand the growing phenomenon of transition among the tribal women and its impact on socio-economic status.

5. This problem has to be studied from different angles. So the one broad and main problem gives rise to many other problems. There are many other reasons for the poor and pitiable conditions of the tribal women. These problems are of so much importance and urgency that they have to be solved and studied.

Objectives:

1. To know the socio-economic profile of the tribal women.

2. To analyze the educational status of tribal girls.

3. To study the nature of economic empowerment and migration and related exploitation of tribal women.

4. To know the extent of crime against tribal women and girls.

5. To evaluate the participation of tribal women in the development programme executed by government.

Universe of the Study

Jharkhand has a population of 26.93 million, consisting of 13.88 million males and 13.08 million females. The sex ratio is 941 females to 1000 males. The population consists of 28% tribal's, 12% Scheduled Castes and 60% others. There are 274 persons for each square kilometer of land. However, the population density varies considerably from as low as 148 per square kilometer in Gumla district to as high as 1167 per square kilometer in Dhanbad district. Around 10% of the population is Bengali speaking and 70% speak various dialects of Hindi.

The tribal population is around 28% of the Jharkhand state, which has been a home to a variety of tribal communities.

The tribes of Jharkhand consist of 32 tribes inhabiting in Jharkhand state of India. The tribes in Jharkhand were originally classified on the basis of their cultural types by the world-renowned Indian anthropologist late Professor L. P. Vidyarthi. His classification was as follows:

1. hunter-gatherer type – Birhor, Korwa, Hill Kharia

2. Shifting Agriculture – Sauria Paharia

3. Simple artisans – Mahli, Lohra, Karmali, Chik Baraik

4. Settled agriculturists – Santhal, Munda, Oraon, Ho, Bhumij etc.

At the district level, Garhwa district has been selected on the basis compared to Jharkhand state such as :

Table : 03.01

Comparison of Development Indicators of Jharkhand and Garhwa

S.N	Indicators	State Jharkhand	District Garhawa
1	Density of Population (Person/ Sq. Km)	338	256
2	Total Literacy Rate	54.13%	30.62%
A	Male Literacy Rate	67.94%	42.62%
B	Female Literacy Rate	39.38%	17.80%
3	Sex Ratio (Female/1000 males)	941	935
4	Total Population	2.62%	3.89%
A	Rural Population	91.72%	95.88%
B	Urban Population	8.28%	4.11%
5	Scheduled Tribes	27.67%	19.91% (Total population 1034151 Census2001)
6	BPL	-	55.3%

The state of Jharkhand, Garhwa district ranks 16th on the basis of literacy rate. Garhwa district comes under the III rd category (those districts in population density and literacy rate both. IV[Th] categories in number of population live in district.

In spite of the universalization of Primary education programme like DPEP (District Primary Education Programme) Garhwa district lags behind the target. Its gross enrolment ratio at elementary level is only 47.5%. 66% of the girls of the district are being married at the age of below 18years. Garhwa is infamous of supplying a large number of child labours to the carpet weaving industries of Utter Pradesh.

Procedure of Sample Selection

Though the Tribals are spread over the entire length and breadth of the state, there are certain districts which have larger concentration of Tribals. Such as Lohardaga, Gumla, Hazaribag, Dumka, Chatra, Latehar, Garhwa etc. Out of them Garhwa district has been selected for the proposed study.

Tribal population of Garhwa district still lives in forest tract. The speed of urbanization has been extremely slow due to rural economy based on agriculture. Total population as per 2001 census has been recorded 1034151. Out of total population of the district, scheduled tribes consist 19.91%. Thus, the total number of scheduled tribes population is approximately 2 lakhs.

"Multi stage sampling method" has been adopted for the proposed study. This district has three subdivisions namely Garhwa Ranka and Nagar – Untari with seven police stations i.e. (1) Garhwa (2) Meral (3) Ranka, (4) Bhandariya (5) Nagar – Untari (6) Bhawanathpur (7) Dhurki. Presently there are 19 blocks in the district such as Kharaundhi, Bhawnathpur, Ramna, Nagar Untari, Dhurki, Kandi, Majhiaon, Danda, Chinia, Meral, Garhwa, Ranka, Ramkanda, Dandai Ketar, Bardiha, Bhandaria, Bishunpura, Sagma. Of them, 12 blocks are those which have the population of primitive tribal groups such as Chinia, Ramakanda, Ranka, Garhwa , Majhiaon, Dhurki, Bhandariya, Nagar Untari, Dandai, Bhawanathpur and Meral.

At the second level of sampling procedure of the 19 blocks (CD) of Garhwa district, two such blocks have been selected which have large concentration of tribal population as compared to other blocks such as Chiniya and Bhandaria.

These blocks have more than 50% tribal population. Chiniya block has 15,273 tribal population out of the total population i.e. 30,790and Bhandaria block has 31,810 tribal population out of total population i.c. 51,488. These blocks have been selected on the basis of purposive sampling procedure.

At the third level of sampling procedure, Bhandariya and chiniya blocks have been selected twenty four (24) primitive tribal villages (As per the primitive tribe group survey 2002-2003) (Jharkhand Tribal Research Institute, Ranchi) The total number of both blocks have been taken as a sample.

Table : 03.02

Names of villages may be revised as some names are not correctly mentined.

Block	Villages	No. Of Families	Block	Villages	No. Of Families
Chiniya	Hetarkala	49	Bhandaria	Hesatu	27
	Hetarkhurd	0.2		Manjari	16
	Masra	51		Sinjo	31
	Parsu	20		Binda	21
	Bilauti	0.9		Chemo	11
	Calbahi	10		Harta	34
	Puregara	20		Hesatu	7
	Rajbans	55		Kokhadih	21
	Chapkali	27		Kulahi	16
	Doal	103		Kuman	6
	Sigsiga	29		Madgari	18
	Rani Chery	48		Manjuri	25
		33		Naoka	58
	Chirka	27		Naoka	6
	Palhe	30		Paat	15
	Khuri	37		Pachayat	47
		44		Parro	17
	Beta	18		Polpol	10
		85		Rodo	7
	Sigsiga Kala	9		Saneya	10
	Kerotia	71		Sangako	5

	Barwadih	52		Saraidih	2
		18		Sarunat	32
		43		Sinjo	7
				Tehri	4
				Tevali	5
				Totaki	3
				Turnera	1
				Turer, Ramar	14, 3
	Total	**880**		**Total**	**479**

Out of these villages shown in table no. (3.02) those villages which have less than ten families have been excluded on the basis of their negligible number. Fifty percent tribal families of remaining villages were chosen as sample unit by using stratified random sampling method. Viewing our special reference to women for this study, female member of the household have been taken as a sample unit. The total number of these females (respondents) is 526 in Bhandariya block and 746 in Chiniya block respectively.

As the Village were selected in each block. Thereafter, small villages, the female heads or the female members of each of the tribal families have been included in the sample.

The tool or Instrument for the study

An Interview schedule designed as to incorporate the main objective of the study. It consists of several sections, each focusing on one important aspect of tribals. Care was taken to order the sections in a logical sequence. The interview scheduled consists of both structured and open ended questions.

Pilot study or pretesting of interview schedule

In order to test the validity and reliability of the field instrument, a pilot study was conducted on 25 households. The purpose of pilot study was also to acquire the researcher with the field situations and build- up a necessary rapport with the community under investigation. The pilot study could reveal some of the

81

shortcomings of the instrument. It could indicate that some of the questions included in the interview schedule were rather ambiguous and needed to be reframed. Based on the experience of the pilot study, the interview schedule was suitably modified to make it more valid and reliable. In addition to this the pilot study also helped the researcher in gaining important insights into the community life of tribals which could enable the researcher to be better prepared to launch the main field work. It revealed that the important aspects of tribal women and their community that need to be probed into are the personal and parental history of the respondent size of the family, marital status, expenditure, saving and investments besides, assets and liabilities, hobbies and culture, traditions, pass time and so forth.

1.   The researcher had prepared an interview schedule of question divided on the basis of different aspects of study for example, the demographic aspect of the sample cases or households, social conditions including the institutions of family, marriage, kinship, divorce, and re- marriage. In the same way, a set of questions was devoted to find out the educational levels and leisure activities of the respondents.

2.   In the next part of the questions, the economic conditions of the respondent are assessed with reference to their landed properties occupations sources of income, and the quantity of income, the level of expenditure etc. In this context some question are posed to realize the sources of loan and the amount of the loan borrowed by the respondent for various purposes. The next part of the interview schedule contained a few questions regarding the development programmes launched by the government and their impact on the tribal women

It was necessary to ask them at the outset whether the respondent are aware of the new programmes and whether they are conscious about the facilities extended for the depressed classes in general and tribal groups in particular.

These are the some variables which have been included in Interview schedule.

Study variables:

- Religion
- Community
- Family Type
- Family Headship
- Age/ Birth order
- Place of birth (Rural/ Urban)
- Marital Status
- Age at marriage
- Education
- Skill Training
- Occupation
- Household Income
- Respondent's Income
- Standard of living
- Membership in SHGs

Dependent Variables used in the study are:

- Responsibilities sharing.
- Decision- making.
- Access and Control over resources.
- Domestic Responsibilities sharing.
- Awareness about social legislations/ women welfare programmes.
- Freedom of articulation, mobility, work, dress and voting.
- Participation in community activities:
- Political participation
- Gender Discrimination
- Male domination
- Violence against women.

Data collection

The research team included one principal investigator, one project fellow and two field investigators one from each block. Field investigators was carefully selected and were all women. The data collectors were well trained and educated and had prior experience of surveys. To ensure safety, arrangements were made for interviewer to travel in pairs, to carry mobile phone to use designated mean of transport or to assign a trusted escort to accompany teams into certain neighborhoods known to be unsafe for women as these are rebel-hit blocks. It was also instructed to avoid conducting interview in the evenings for the same purpose. Elected representatives were informed earlier to ensure cooperation of the local bodies.

Frame Work of Data Analysis

The data collected from primary and secondary sources were carefully scrutinized and transcribed before the commencement of data tabulation and interpreted through statistical tools.

Descriptive statistical tools like frequency, percentage, mean, and ratio are used to analyze the primary data. The analyzed data were presented in the form of tables, Data of the sample villages has reflected only in the study for analysis. i.e. literacy rate.

Data Processing

The interview schedules administered on migrant tribal women and girls were edited, codified and tabulated. Data processing was carried out with the help of computers. The data analysis was planned in such a way that possible errors during data processing would be excluded. Numerical symbols were assigned to the responses in the interview schedule yielding a total of 58 variables. Computers were also used for statistical analysis of the data. In the first instance sorting was done to generate frequency tables for each independent variable. The report that follows incorporates the data, analysis, the interpretation and the inferences draw there from.

Report Presentation

The research work along with data processing and analysis including the introduction and conclusion is covered under following chapters:

Chapter 1: Status of Tribal in India

Chapter one attempts to highlight the tribal phenomenon like definition, characteristics, distribution of tribal population, constitutional and legislative Provisions, reservation policies, their distribution, their classification, major tribal communities in India, tribal population in Jharkhand, growth rate, tribal women in Jharkhand and development programmes for the benefit of tribals.

Chapter 2: Overview of Literature

This chapter deals with the major operational definitions and meaning terms under study, review of international level study, review of national level study.

Chapter 3: Objectives and Study Design

This chapter deals with the objectives and study design, consisting of the statement of problem, objectives, sampling variables, tools and methods of data collection, analysis of framework and limitations of the study.

Chapter 4: Profile of Study Area and Social Status of Respondents

This chapter deals with the study about the research area and social status of respondents and educational status of tribal women.

Chapter 5: Economic Status of Respondents

This chapter has analysed the livelihood conditions, occupations, house type, farming conditions and indebtedness.

Chapter 6: Work Participation, Gender Discrimination and Exploitation

This chapter has analysed the work load of tribal women, migration problems, exploitation at work place and discrimination.

Chapter 7: Health status, Political Organisation

This chapter deals with the health related problems, health awareness, political and decision making power of tribal women.

Chapter 8: Conclusions and Suggestions

Major findings of seven chapters are included in this chapter and suggestions are given on the basis of findings. Bibliography and appendices is included.

Limitation of the Study

1.   The study included only selected tribal women who are covered under Major Projects. The Villages outside Major Projects are not included which could have enabled to draw better inference about the selected tribal women.

2.   The study is location specific characterized by local economic and livelihood condition. Thus it may not have same application in other location.

3.   It may so happen that the growth rate of the population may differ from the growth rate of the sample due to possible error in expression of the opinion by the sample.

4.   Data is perfect to the extent to being honest response of the sample. The recall method of data collection for some variables may not be very much perfect.

5.   The opinion of the sample may not fully reflect the opinion of the same tribal women of other district.

6.   Due to the seasonal migration, the sample unit may differ as selected villages under study.

REFERENCES

Banu. Zenab   (2001) :'Tribal Women Empowerment and Gender Issues', Kanishka
                   publishers New Delhi
                   Census Report 2001.

Coulsent .et.al. (eds)   (1963) :'Oxford Illustrated Dictionary', Landon, Oxford university
                   Press.

Harsankar and Laxmi Devi   :'The Tribes and their Development', current publications Agara
                   page 13 15.

Kailash   (1993) :"Tribal Education and Occupation. Dynamics of import and
                   change", Manak Publications 176.

Majumadar, D.N   (1958) :'Outed in Vidyarthi', LP & Rai, BK (1977) Tribal cultural of
                   India: Concept Delhi, Report on Nfsh-2-1998-99 Jharkhand state.

Theodorson, George A. &

theodorsom Achilles G. (1969) :'A Modern Dictionary of Sociology, Methuen & co Ltd, London.

Taylor, B.E   (1988):'Dictionary of Anthropology (special Indian Edition)', Delhi
                   Goyal Saab Publication and Distributors.

87

CHAPTER – IV

ABOUT THE DISTRICT AND PROFILE OF TRIBAL WOMEN

The erstwhile Garhwa Sub-division of Palamau district comprising was separated from Palamu district as an independent district "Garhwa" with effect from 1st April 1991.It is situated on Southwest corner of Palamu division, which lies between 23° 60'and 24° 39'N latitude and 83° 22' and 84° 00' longitude. The district is surrounded by river Sone in the north; Palamu district and area of Chhattisgarh in the south; Palamu district in the east and Sarguja district of Chhattisgarh and Sonebhadra district of U.P.in the west. Garhwa district falls under Palamu Commissionery consisting of 19 blocks and three subdivisions namely Garhwa Ranka and Nagar-Untrai At the time of new district of Garhwa, there were eight old blocks namely :-

Blocks

(1). Garhwa (2). Meral (3). Ranka (4). Bonhandariya (5). Majhiaon (6). Nagar-Untari (7). Bhawnathpur and (8). Dhurki. Later 6 new blocks were created from old blocks on administrative ground namely (1). Dandai (2). Chiniya (3). Kharoundhi (4). Ramna (5). Ramkanda and (6). Kandi Later 5 new blocks were also created from old 14 blocks on administrative ground namely 1. Danda 2. Ketar 3. Bishunpura 4. Bardiha and 5. Sagma.

So presently there are 19 blocks in Garhwa district. There are 196 gram panchayats. 916 inhabited villages and 62 un-inhabited (Bechiragi) villages in this district The district has two police sub-division named Garhwa and Nagar-Untrai. With eight polic station i.e.

1. Garhwa	2. Meral	3. Ranka	4. Bhandariya	5.Majhiyaon
6. Nagar-Untari	7. Bhawnathpur and		8. Dhurki	9. Danda
10. Ramkanda	11. Bishunpura	12. Dandai	13. Kandi	14. Ramna
15. Ketar	16. Sagma	17. Chinia	18. Kharaundhi	19. Bardiha

The district has only one Municipal town at Garhwa head quarter. The Municipal town has a brief history. On 6th May? Garhwa Union Board was created under the village administration Act of 1992 when it became Union Board. The board consisted of five elected and two nominated members and they worked under part-IV of the above-mentioned Act. The Union Board administered the function of conservancy and sanitation including drainage in local area, street lighting and prevention of public nuisance there in On 9th August 1957 Garhwa Union Board was abolished and in its place a Notified Area Committee (NAC) was established as per the Government Notification no.6991-L.S.G., dated 14th June 1957. The N.A.C. area consisted of eight villages; Garhwa (Thana No.-339), Tandawa (Thana No. 338), Sahijana (Thana No.-345), Dipawa (Thana No.-341), Ngawa (Thana No.-340), Pipara Kala (Thana No.-342), Unchari (Thana No.-241) and Sonpurwa (Thana No.-242,) Later this N.A.C. got the status of Municipality. It has been working as Municipality since 15 August 1972.

Early History

The early history of this district depends on the history of Palamu district. The district consisted mostly of forest tracts. The timothy seldom attracted the attention of invading armies. So the area remained outside the pale of dominating empires In the past the area was probably inhabited by tribal people. It is believed that the three aboriginal races viz the Kharwars, the Oraons and Cheroes practically reigned over this tract. The Cheroes reigned over Garhwa for nearly 200 years from sixteen century to onwards. The most famous among Chero rulers was Medani Rai.

1857 Movement

Regarding 1857 Movement it has been observed by Historian P.C.Roy Chaudhari – "But the district that was most affected was Palamu. The movement at Palamu was of very different character from Mere of the Sepoys. The indigenous population of the district consisting of the Cheroes, Bhoktas and Kharwars had taken to arms. Practically the bulk of Jagirdars and Zamindars had sided against and Pitamber Sah. Nalambar and Pitambar both brother and leader of the Kharawar tribes, declared themselves independent and created haboc for Britishers. Later many other Jagirdars and people joined them. Later Nilambar and Pitambar Sah were captured by the British army and movement ended with their arrest. Garhwa played a significant role in freedom movement of the country.

Natural Formation

The average elevation of Garhwa district is about 1200 feet above the sea level. The hills in the district are widely scattered. There are also low land in Northern and Western parts of the district which are suitable for agricultural purposes. The hill which is called Gulgupath is well worth a visit by the hikers. The village is occupied mostly by Korwas, a tribal people.

River System

The general line of drainage is from south to north towards the river Koyal and Sone. Koyal forms the eastern boundary and Sone forms northern boundary of the district. There are also a host of smaller, most of which are from mountain currents with rock stream beds. Other important rivers of the district are Danro, Sarsatiya, Tahale, Annaraj, Urea, Bai Banki, Bellaiti, Pando, Biraha, and Sapahi. Other notable river is Kanhar which covers south eastern boundary of the district for about 80 km. Due to its geographical formation, Garhwa district is rich in water resources.

Climate Condition

The climate of this district is on the whole dry and bracing. The year can be divided in three main seasons, the winter season from November to March, the summer season from March to May and Monsoon. The average annual rainfall of the district as a whole is 1.335 mm/ 52.55 inches. From the onset of the Monsoon by the middle of June, rainfall rapidly increases reaching the peak level in August. The annual variation of rainfall is not much. December and January are coolest months. By March temperature begins to rise steadity. In May and early part of June the

90

maximum temperature can be as high as 47^0 C on individual days. Humidity is generally normal in this district, except in monsoon months.

Land Use and Crops

Garhwa lies partially under rain shadow area and often haunted by drought. Although yearly average rainfall is sufficient for agriculture work but unequal distribution of seasonal rain affects the main crops badly. During summer season water level of the district goes down and most of the villages have to face scarcity of water. Due to drought a section of agricultural labour migrates every year to nearby districts of other states for employment and livelihood. But due to the govts. various development scheme. and Minor & Major irrigational work in recent years, agricultural work has development to a large extent. Rice is the main staple food of the district and it is chiefly grown. Maize and wheet are other notable crops. Sugarcane, oilseeds, pulses and vegetables are also grown in the district. The seed collection of sal, mahua, semal and other forest product like lac, tendu leaves, etc. are also part of income for some period. There are 37530.50 Hectare of agriculture land in the district. Approximately per capita land holding is 0.17 Hectare.

Demographic profile

The Garhwa district is primarily rural and most of the population resides in villages Tribal population of the district still lives in forest tract. The speed of urbanization has been extremely slow due to rural economy based on agriculture. Total population of the district as per 1991 census was 801239 . in 2001 census the population of district was recorded 991492 as against the urban population of 42659 in urban population Garhwa municipality has recorded 36708 and sinduria (Bhawnathpur) has been recorded 5951 souls form previous census 1991 to present census 2001; the rate of urban growth of this district had been 53.72 percent which is second highest in Jharkhand state after Godda district. The percentage of decadal growth (1991-2001) of the district, scheduled caste formed 26.32 % and scheduled tribe 19.91%

The sex ratio is adverse for females in Garhwa like other district of Jharkhand Garhwa has a sex ratio of 935:1000 in rural areas which is 938 female against 1000 male and in urban areas 864 female against 1000 male.

Civil Surgeon Cum C.M.O. Office Garhwa : 01

Additional C.M.O. - Office Garhwa : 01

Sub Divisional Health Centers : 01

Primary Health Centers : **10**

- Garhwa Sadar : Danda
- Bhawnathpur : Ramkanda
- Dhurki : Manjhiaon
- Meral : Nagar Untari
- Ranka : Kandi

Community Health Centers : **09**

- Garhwa Sadar : Garhwa Urban
- Bhawanthpur : Bhandaria
- Dhurki : Majhiaon
- Meral : Nagar Untari
- Ranka

Health Sub Centers : 111

Village Health Committee : 859

Maternal Health Analysis

As per the CHC report for the period April 09 to March 2010, 26644 pregnant women were registered for ANC checkup which is 77.69% of the targeted pregnant women. But only 19.15% pregnant women were registered in the trimester. 15908 women received 3 ANC checkups which was only 46.39% of targeted women population. 1010 (2.95%) pregnant women were identified as anemic. In the year April to September 2010 there were 15485 (89.64%) pregnant women registered while only 2882 (16.68%) were registered in their first trimester. Only 9716 (56.25%) pregnant women got 3 ANC checkups.

Table : 04.01

Ante Natal Care (ANC) at Community Health Centers

Total	Achievement Apr09-Mar09	Achievement Apr10-Mar10
Pregnant Population	34295	17274
Regd. For 1 trimester	6566	2882
Regd. for 1 ANC	26644	15485
Women with 3 ANC Checkups	15908	9716
Women with Anemia	1010	658
Women with PNC	7143	4479
Institutional Delivaries	6021	3329
Delivaries at CHCs	5896	3260
Received 100 IFA tabets	21255	11990
BCG Percentage	687	352
DPT-I Percentage	1059	338
DPT-III Percentage	725	289
Measles Percentage	648	333
Fully Immunization %	628	320

DAs per the CHC date it shows that in the year April 09 to March 10, there were 21255 (61.98%) pregnant women who received 100 IFA and 6021 (20.83%) underwent PNC care within 48 hours of delivery. There were 6021 deliveries conducted in govt. CHCs and other private health institutions where 5896 (97.92%)

deliveries were conducted under govt. health facilities. 5413 (91.81%) women received MMJSSA incentive money during the services in April to the Sept.2010.

Table : 04.02

Family planning at Community Health Centers

Total	Achievement Apr09-Mar09	Achievement Apr10-Mar10
Oral Pills Distributed	32621	12602
Condoms Distributed	319752	133386
Femaale Sterilization	6105	1401
Non-scalpel Vasectomy	43	126

School Health

In the progress of school health programme the HSC wise the micro plan has been made in all the schools. The health cards to the students have been provided and the regular checkup is being done. Till the date 590 School have been covered out of 1422.

Zilla Parished

Zill Parishad is a local govermment body at the district level in Indian. It loks after the administration of the rural area of the district and its office is located at the district headquarters. The Hindi word Parishad means Council and Zilla Parishad translates into District Council. Members of the Zilla Parishad are elected from the district on the basis of adult franchise for a term of five years. Zilla Parishad has minimum 50 and maximum 75 members. Seats are reseved for Scheduled Castes, Scheduled Tribes, backward classes and women. The Chaimen of all the Panchayat Samitis are elected by the members of Zilla Parishad. The Parishad is headed by a parishad and a Vice- parishad. The chief Executive Officer (CEO), who is anchal IAS officer, heads the administrative machinery of the Zilla Parishad. The CEO supervises the divisions of the Parishad and executes its development schemes.

Functions

- Provide essential services and facilities to the rural population and the planning and execution of the development programmes for the district.
- Supply improved seeds to farmers. Inform them about new techniques of training. Undertake construction of small-scale irrigation projects and percolation of tanks. Maintain pastures and grazing lands.
- Set up and run schools in villages, execute programmes for adult literacy and run libraries.
- Start Primary Health Centers (PHCs) and hospitals in villages, mobile hospitals for hamlets, vaccination drives against epidemics and family welfare campaigns.
- Construct bridges and roads.
- Execute plans for the development of scheduled castes and scheduled tribes. Run ashram for adivasi children. Set up free hostels for scheduled caste and scheduled tribe students.
- Encourage entrepreneurs to start small-scale industries like cottage industries, handicraft, agriculture produce processing mills, dairy farms, etc. Implement rural employment schemes.
- They construct roads, school, & public properties and take care of the public properties.
- They even provide work for the poor people. (tribes, scheduled caste, lower caste)

Development schemes

MGNREGA, BRGF, IAY, SGSY, Integrated Action Plan (IPA), Social Security, Public Distribution System (PDS), Health & Family Welfare, ICDS, Sarwa Siksha Abhiyan, RSBY.

Basic data sheet of Garhwa district

Population:

Persons	1,035,464	Number of households	174,264
Males	535,332	Household size (per household)	6
Females	500,132		
Growth (1991 - 2001)	29.05	Sex ratio (Females per 1000 males)	934
Rural	992,825	Sex ratio (0-6 years)	962
Urban	42,639		
Scheduled Caste population	247,280		Scheduled
Tribe population	158,959		
Percentage to total population	Percentage	23.88	to
total population		15.35	

Literacy and Educational level

Literates		Educational Level attained	
Persons	317,078	Total	317,078
Males	228,151	Without level	13,092
Females	88,927	Below primary	100,712
Literacy rate		Primary	92,857
Persons	39.21	Middle	48,324
Males	54.36	Matric /Higher Secondary/Diploma	51,170
Females	22.87	Graduate and above	10,916

Workers		Age groups	
Total workers	402,921	0 - 4 years	150,755
Main workers	231,057	5 - 14 years	309,986
Marginal workers	171,864	15 - 59 years	505,880
Non-workers	632,543	60 years and above (Incl. A.N.S.)	68,843

Scheduled Castes (Largest three)		Scheduled Tribes (Largest three)	
1.Chamar etc.	88,954	1.Kharwar	72,632
2.Bhuiya	66,548	2.Oraon	41,726
3.Dusadh etc.	47,932	3.Korwa	19,234

Religions (Largest three)

Amenities and infrastructural facilities

1.Hindus	867,775	Total inhabited villages	858
2.Muslims	149,102		
3.Christians	12,353	Amenities available in villages	
		No. of villages	
		Drinking water facilities	858
		Safe Drinking water	849
Important Towns (Largest three)		Electricity (Power Supply)	190
Population		Electricity (domestic)	139
		Electricity (Agriculture)	58
1.Garhwa (M)	36,686	Primary school	566
2.Sinduria (CT)	5,953	Middle schools	155
		Secondary/ Sr. Secondary schools	42
		College	2
House Type		Medical facility	116
		Primary Health Centre	18
		Primary Health Sub-Centre	54

Type of house (% of households occupying)

Post, telegraph and telephone facility 126

Permanent	8.9	Bus services	99
Semi-permanent	90.4	Paved approach road	180
Temporary	0.7	Mud approach road 8 00Source	

Social Background of the Tribal Women

The socio-economic background of an individual, to a large extent, determines his early socialization, shapes his personality and influences his day to day interaction with other members of the community. Socio-economic background, in fact, places an individual in a   specific position within his community and shapes his behavioral pattern in course of time. The values and personal convictions of a person are very much influenced by the environment to which he is exposed from the very beginning. The understanding of a man's early socio-economic environment is, therefore, essential for a proper understanding of his behavior and actions *(Singh, R.S., 1985, p. 66)*.

Family

The sociologists have defined family structure in terms of nuclear and joint family *(Desai, A.R., 1969, pp. 31-32)*. The joint family is larger in size. The tribal usually have joint family system. The members of the joint families include grand parents, their children and grand children including the unmarried female members of the family. For a theoretical analysis of the institution of family, the common points taken into account including marriage, sex, kinship, economy and culture. The bureau of census defines family as a group of two or more persons related to blood, marriage or adoption etc. All such persons are considered as member of one family. According to Rad Chiffe Brown (quoted by Lowie, 1956) the "elementary form of family includes a single husband and wife with their child or children; this latter relationship to be understood in a sociological rather than a physiological Sence". According to Maciver and page (1957)," the family is a group defined by sex relationship sufficiently precise and enduring to provide for the procreating and upbringing children and it may include collateral or subsidiary relationships, but it is constituted by the living together of mates forming which their offspring a distinctive unity" *(sahay , k.k., 2005.p.135)*.

Types of family in both blocks of Garhwa district is shown in the following table.

Table : 04.03
The Type of Family Women live in

Family	Chiniya	Bhandariya	Total
Nuclear	486	204	690
Joint Family	260	322	582
Total	746	526	1272

The above table (no. 04.03) shows, that 54.24% tribal women belonged to nuclear family whereas 45.75% of respondents have joint family background. The institution of joint family has deep roots in the Indian tradition and culture. However, owing to the inflow of western individualistic attitudes of life and impact of urbanization, the joint family system has come under heavy strain. It is sometimes held that the environment of joint family is not always conducive for development of the total personality of an individual.

Age

Table : 04.04

Age distribution of the Tribal Women

Age group	Chiniya	Bhandariya	Total
18-25	156	96	252 (19.81%)
26-35	294	184	478 (37.57%)
36-45	224	174	398 (31.28%)
46-55	56	46	102 (8.01%)
56-65	12	22	34 (2.67%)
66-75 and above	4	4	8 (0.62%)
Total	746 (58.65%)	526 (41.36%)	1272 (100%)

99

As the above table 4.4 shows, that there is difference in age composition between the respondents of Chiniya and Bhandariya while. The highest number of the respondents 37.57% are between 26 to 35 of age, 31.28% Respondents are between 36 to 45 of age. Significantly, 19.81% Respondents are between the age 18 to 25. The Respondents who were above the age of 50 years constituted 2.67% of the total population. 8.01% Respondents are between the age of 46 to 55 and only 0.62% Respondents are between the age of 66 to 75. The above analysis shows that out of the total population, middle age women are more dominant in making the family size more relevant.

Caste wise

Caste is significant factor in Indian social structure as the meaningful study is not possible without its being taken into consideration.

Table : 04.05

Sub-Caste wise distribution of the Tribal Women

Scheduled tribes	Chiniya	Bhandariya	Total
Kharwar	442	508	950 (74.69%)
Parahiya	106	0	106 (8.34%)
Korwa	80	10	90 (7.08%)
Other tribes	118	8	126 (9.91%)
Total	**746 (58.65%)**	**526 (41.36%)**	**1272 (100%)**

As the above table no 4.5 shows that out of the total selected tribes,74.69%respondents belong to kharwar sub-tribe, 8.34%respondents belong to parahiya sub-tribe, 7.08%respondents belong to korwa sub tribe and only 9.91% respondents belong to other sub-tribes in which only a few tribes were found in selected area of research.

The major characteristics of sub tribes found in this study are given below.

Kharwar

The population of the kharwars is 1,92,024, which is 2.70% of the total tribal population. They are mainly concentrated in Palamu, Ranchi, Hazaribagh, etc. Majority of them live in palamu. dalton has opined that there has been traditional connection between the Cheros and kharwars who are said to have invaded Palamu from Rohtas and drove the local Rajput chief out of the region.

Family

The family is the smallest unit of the society. It is nuclear in structure that consist of husband, wife and their unmarried children. The joint families are rare. The married sons start living with their wives and start separate family. the girls don't inherit the property of the father so, they are not expected to look after their aged parents. The family is patrianchal the father is the head of the family but for the smooth functioning of the family, they follow the division of labour based on age and sex. The cooking and the household management lies with the mother, while the father does the outside management the daughter extend help to their mother and sons and also extend cooperation to their father.

Marriage

The marriage is very important ritual, which comes in the life of both boys and girls, if they are sexually valid . Even the sexually invalid persons are also married to wash the stain of unmarried ness, which is not taken good in the society. Divorced life is taken good in comparison to unmarried life. The usual form of marriage is monogamy. Marriage, outside the tribes is not permissible they practice pologamy, exogamy which forbids intermarriage in certain degree of collateral relationship. Widow remarriage is permissible.

They have their own community panchayats in which all the male elders of the village participate. A number of village are grouped in a chata and its head is known as pradhan. Head of panchayat name is mukhiya.

Relgion

The religion of the kharwar presents a mixture of tribal and Hindu religion. Their main gods and goddesses rare singbonga, lakshmi, bhagvati, durga, hanuman, gram bonga, dihwar bonga, etc.. They also believe in sprits, bhuta-preta and witch craft bhuta-preta is driven out by witch docter they also do a number of totaka to neutrilize the attack of evil spirit, bhuta –preta and witch craft. They also observe a number of taboos for their wellbeing of the family members.

Festivals

The kharwars follow the local bhahmansinghi and also the local tribal religious ceremonies and festivals. They celebrate festibals like chhath, sarhul durga puja, diwali, jitia, sohrai, nawakhani, phagu and ramnaumi.

Death

The kharwars are well aware of the death. They believe that death is associated with every birth, but there is difference between death and the death in old hood is taken as good because it transforms the old body into new one either as ancestor or as rebirth.

Death brings pollution for nine days. The pollution is observed at lineage and clan level. No family belonging to the lineage and clan group of the dead, use oil and turmeric in food. They do not do any auspicious work during the period. Male members don't do shaving during ninth days. All family wash their houses, country yard, clothes, utensils. After that they touch oil and turmeric and become clean. The male member do shaving of head, beard and mustache.

The Korwa

The korwas are kolarian tribes found in Surguja and Jashpur district of Chhattisgarh and Palamu. The population of korwas is 27,177. A village consists of several groups and ties of blood link the members of a group to one another korwas

102

also have both village panchayat and clan panchayat. The former look after the inner village disputes while the latter ensure that the social codes are followed properly. For instance if an individual marries outside the tribe, he is declared an outcast They have seven clans like raj korwa, manraji, samat, edgi, muruang, birjia, and birhor. Each sub-caste is obliged to marry among themseveles.

Family

The korwas family is nuclear consisting of a couple and their unmarried children. The married children live in separate house after marriage and establish a separate family. The family is patriarchal. For proper and smooth functioning of the family, the division of labour based on age and sex is prevalent. For example cooking is female specific, while hunting and ploughing is male specific. Girls assist their mother in households chores. The boy assist their father in forest and field they also work as reja (labour)to get wages and increase family income. Males also know how to cook food. Each family member take part in the production and consume according to their needs.

Marriage

There are two types of marriage system-the runaway or love marriage and the second system is arranged marriage in which the father of the boy sends two men of his caste to the girl's father and ask for his daughter. The marriage is arranged after getting consent. One korwa is allowed to keep more than three wives. Ploygamy is permited when the first wife is childless.

Religion

The korwas, like other tribes, worship many deities. Their most important deities are the (supreme god), pat Deota and village deities. They are known as the baiga priest who propitiates them on behalf of the people. They also worship their ancestors. They worship moon, earth, dihwar, gonhal, salsbhani, karma, sarhul. Hadia (rice beer) is their common drink and is served on all special occasions. But now they have started taking local wines, which is easily available in the village markets.

Death

On death, a person is buried in the village burial ground kaman ceremony takes place on the tenth day when all the villagers irrespective of their caste or tribe are invited to participate. The korwas show great reverence for the dead. They are remembered during all the festivals and ceremonies. When social offering are made to them.

Family size

The importance and place of family as a social institution is widely known and perfectly established from the point of view of its content structure as well as function in all social system. But commonly accepted concepts apart from the nature of familiar structure is not always uniform and static but is rather flexible and subject to variation, depending upon and conditioned by the nature of the social ground and consequently the social system in force.. A big joint family has, sometimes more than one hearth or fireplace in a house and the total number of members may go up to 20-30 in a family. It is usually believed that a member of a large family has an advantage over others as he is assured of all-round support from his own family. Besides, in a larger family, some elder members usually get enough time for participation in the village affairs.

Table : 04.06

Family size of the Tribal Women

Response	Chiniya	Bhandariya	Total
Female	848	634	1482
Male	828	590	1418
Boys	1486	872	2358
Girls	1380	820	2200
Total	**4542**	**2916**	**7458**

According to the table no. 04.06, the total population of both blocks are 60.91% and 39.10% respectively. While the size of the family of respondents is not a big family (39.10%) in Bhandariya block, 60.91% of the respondents families was found in Chiniya block. 31.62% respondents were boys and 29.50% were girls out of the total population. 19.88% respondents were female and 19.02% population were male. The present investigation reveals that the big size family have significant co-relation with role of the female and responsibilities in the family at large level.

Education

Educated person is likely to be more adaptive to the changing socio-economic environment and better understand the process of new institutions. In the eye of the villagers, the educated persons are accorded certain degree of status and admiration as they have better contact with the outside world. They are expected to have better knowledge about official procedures, rules and regulations. *(karlo, Rejir 2005, p47).* Education is not only a means of adjustment into the society and allround development, but it is also an end in itself. Education affords perfection to life, and it is closely associated with socio-economic development.

In order to understand the education level in tribes of selected blocks in present study, respondents were asked whether they are educated or not following table is present in this way.

Table : 04.07

Educational level of the Tribal Women

Educational Level	Chiniya	Bhandariya	Total
Illiterate	378	326	704 (55.35%)
Literate	262	136	398 (31.29%)
Primary	060	020	80 (6.29%)
Secondary	030	026	56 (4.41%)
High School	016	018	34 (2.68%)
Total	746 (58.65%)	526 (41.36%)	1272 (100%)

The above table 04.07 reveals that 55.35% of respondents are Illiterate. For the purpose of our study a person who simply can write and sign his name was considered as literate, that is why the literacy percentage is 31.29. While 6.29% respondents were primary level educated, 4.41% respondents were secondary level educated and only 2.68% respondents were high school pass out. Due to lack of facilities of education and low income, respondents were not able to access the education. Another reason is that school are very far away from their place. The percentage of literate in Bhandariya block is comparatively low from Chiniya block. Bhandariya block has high percentage of illiterate. Hence, there is a co-relationship between knowledge, awareness and education.

Marriage

Marriage is an important event in one's life, as it entails turning points from the social and economic points of view. Marital status of the respondents is another important aspect of study in the context of their social life. The following table pertains to marital status of the respondents. There are no respondents who are unmarried.

Early marriages are quite common among all the sub-castes of the tribal women. The reasons are obvious. They do not care for education. Therefore, they do not postpone their marriage. Secondly, they believe that if the marriage takes place at an early age, the husband and wife get into better understanding with each other and cherish love and affection at an early age. The third reason perhaps, may be that by marriage one more member is added to the household to work and to add to the income of the family, as it is customary with all the males and females to participate in the economic activities *(Harsurkar R. Laxmi Devi . 2005., p115).*

Table : 04.08

Marital status of the Tribal Women

Marital status	Chiniya	%	Bhandariya	%	Total
Married	646	86.59	446	84.79	1092 (85.85%)
Widow	94	12.60	80	15.20	174 (13.68%)
Abandoned	6	00.80	0	0	6 (00.48%)
Divorced	0	0	0	0	0
Total	746 (58.65%)	100.00	526 (41.36%)	100.00	1272 (100%)

It is found from the fact as table no. 04.08 shows that majority (85.85%) of the respondents were married. Out of the total population 13.68% respondents were widow. Only 0.48% respondents are abandoned in the comparison of both blocks. Out of the total population of the Bhandariya block 84.79% respondents were found married. Only 15.20% respondents were widow. When it comes facts about Chiniya block out of the total population 86.59% respondents were married whereas 12.60% respondents were found widow. Negligible number of respondent were found abandoned out of the total population and no respondents were divorcee.

REFERENCES

➢ Choudhary, D. S., (1981) :'Emerging Rural Leadership in an Indian State', Manthan
Publication, New Delhi, p. 45.

➢ Desai, A. R.,   (1969) :'Rural Sociology in India', Popular Prakashan, Bombay,
pp. 31-32.

➢ Dharshankar,   (1979) :'Leadership in Panchayat Raj', Panchsheel Prakashan, Jaipur,
pp. 89-90.

➢ http://garhwa.nic.in/pds.html

➢ Harsurkar, R. &   (2005) :'The tribes and their development', Current Publication,
Laxmi Devi,   Agra. p80.

➢ Kalgi. B. B.,   (2008) :'The Scheduled tribes in transition', Classical publishing
company. New Delhi. p120.

➢ Karlo, Rejir.   (2005) :'Emerging pattern of tribal leadership in arunachal Pradesh',
Commen wealth. New Delhi, p47.

➢ Devasia, V. V.   (2003) :'A research study on migrant tribal women girls in ten cities: a
study of their socio-cultural and economic reference to social
intervention', Report of Planning Commission, New Delhi.

➢ Singh, R. S.   (1985) :'Rural Elite, Entrepreneurship and Social Change', Rawat
Publication, Jaipur, p. 66,68.

➢ Sahay, K. K.,   (2005) :'development of gond tribes in modern perspective', Classical
Publishing company. New Delhi, p.135.

➢ Sikligar, P. C., (2006) :'Empowerment of tribal women wavli', Mangal deep
Publications jaipur, p92.

➢ Verma, B. M.,   (1981) :'Rural Leadership in a welfare Society', Manthan Publication,
New Delhi, p. 61.

CHAPTER – V
ECONOMIC STATUS OF THE RESPONDENTS

If there is any field where the tribal are at their worst, it is the field of their economy. Their economic conditions are so miserable that even today they are not able to cope with the general society in spite of many economic development programmes floated by the government especially for the tribal. Their traditional occupations cannot provide them adequate economic means. They have to seek for some additional sources of income. These additional sources depend upon their geographical and social conditions. The nature of economic pursuits may, many times, not only differ from tribe, but even within the same tribe. Different sections might follow different occupations and different economy (Kalgi.b.b., 2008.120).

Ineptness and exploitation grew faster in an atmosphere of ignorance prevailing in tribal communities. Even the bride-price, which the tribals previously paid in kind, is now decided through cash payments. In certain tribal communities the value of bride-price has gone up high as rupees two thousand. For a tribal family, in general, it is highly difficult to manage for this price from its own resources. The same is true in case of expenses on a death feast. Most of them approach the money-lenders and incur debt for such purposes. There are many other rituals and ceremonies connected to birth, death and house construction. Their performance requires money which a large number of people are unable to manage by themselves. It is not only compulsion of various needs, but also the convenience which makes a tribal go to the nearest financing agency, that is, the local money-lenders (Kalgi.b.b.,2008.121)..

Occupation

The economic status of a person plays a crucial role played by the respondents in the family. To ascertain the economic status of the respondents, variables like occupation, annual income, source of income, property, land holding, type of dwelling house etc. were analysed. In addition to this variables, some specific questions were asked to the respondents regarding the luxurious amenities availed by the respondents (Karlo. 2005.58).

Table : 05.01

Distribution of the Tribal Women according of their Occupation

Occupation	Chiniya	Bhandariya	Total
Agriculture	724	204	928 (27.21%)
Labour	708	194	902 (26.45%)
Animals Husbandry	692	186	878 (25.74%)
Others	304	034	338 (9.91%)
Handicraft	216	034	250 (7.33%)
Traditional work	078	034	112 (3.28%)
Home rent	002	000	2 (0.05%)

Note: Total number of respondents is not shown in the table as the same respondents were engaged in more than one occupation. So, total number exceeds the actual number of respondents.

The above table 05.01 reveals that 27.21% of the respondents are engaged in agriculture, as it is the main occupation of the respondents. 26.45% respondents are engaged in labour work. 25.74% respondents of the total population are engaged in animals husbandry. The proportion of respondents whose main occupation was agriculture are also engaged in handicraft and traditional work or occupation with 7.33% and 3.28% respectively. While it is comparatively lesser in case of home rent. The data of this particular table shows that occupation is not a significant factor in assessing the economic status of the respondents but it has important role in defining

110

the status of the tribal women in family. In relation to above table income of respondents by various occupation have been shown in next table.

Income of respondents

Income was the second factor in our study to determine the economic status of the respondents. Many studies have indicated that there is positive relationship between income and status. (chaudhary, 1981.54). For the purpose of our study, the respondents were asked about their annual income in rupees. Since most of the tribal women did not have permanent source of income, it was not feasible to determine their exact annual income. That is why, their income was categorized into ranges viz., low income group (Below 5000), moderate income group (6000-15000), high income group (16000-25000), and very high income group (26000-35000).

Table : 05.02

The income mentioned over here on the basis of the revelation made by the Tribal Women themselves.

Income in Rs.	Chiniya	Bhandariya	Total
Below to 5000	12	334	346 (27.20%)
6000-15000	282	74	356 (27.98%)
16000-25000	434	118	552 (43.39%)
26000-35000	18	0	18 (1.41%)
Total	**746**	**526**	**1272 (100%)**

The table 05.02 reveals that majority (43.39%) of the respondents belongs to the high income group, followed by the respondents belongs to moderate income group (27.98%), low income group (27.20%), and very high income group is 1.41%. Thus, this study shows that income has been defined the economic status of respondents. The comparative analysis of the income of the respondents of both blocks, Chiniya and Bhandariya reveals that respondents of Bhandariya block belong to low income group. There was no respondent found belonging to very high income group. Thus, this study shows that the respondents of the Chiniya block are slightly better in terms of the monitary income.

Land holding

The economic status of a person is not assessed by income alone but other indicators of wealth like land holding as well is equally important. Such indicator of economic status has greater relevance in the traditional economy where the income in term of rupees is negligible as well as difficult to ascertain. It was observed during the course of interview that considerable number of respondents were hesitant to disclose their income and tended to conceal the exact income. Thus, income alone can not determine the economic status. It may lack accuracy and reliability for meaningful conclusion.

Table : 05.03

Distributions of the Tribal Women showing land holding

Land ownership	Chiniya	Bhandariya	Total
0-1 acres	132	262	394 (30.98%)
2-3 acres	416	134	550 (43.24%)
4-5 acres	142	20	162 (12.74%)
6 -7 acres	10	8	18 (1.43%)
8-9 acres	-	4	4 (0.31%)
10 acres & above	-	18	18 (1.42%)
Landless family	46	80	126 (9.91%)
Total	746 (58.65%)	526 (41.36%)	1272 (100%)

On the basis of above table 05.03 it reveals that 43.24% respondents possess 2-3 acres land ownership. 30.98% respondents have 0-1 acres or less land ownership. 12.74% respondents have 4-5 acres land ownership. 1.43% respondents have 6-7 acres land ownership. It is shown in the table that only in Bhandariya block 0.31% have 8-9 acres land ownership. And 1.42% respondents have 10 acres & above land ownership. It is important to mention here that 9.91% respondents do not have any kind of land ownership.

Type of Dwelling house

The Type of dwelling house of the respondents is considered as one of the reliable indicator of respondent's socio economic status because the investigators visited their house for interview. So, there was no scope for manipulation of the facts by the respondents. It was found that majority of the respondents lived in cachucha house or traditional thatched house. Most of the tribal in India live in huts constructed by using locally available material like grass, bamboos, wooden logs and mud. Bricks and Cement are rarely used. The following table shows the type of dwelling house of the respondents.

Table : 05.04

Type of houses of the Respondents

Type of construction of house	Chiniya	Bhandariya	Total
Pucca	34	12	46 (3.62%)
Kachcha	642	472	1114 (87.58%)
Semi- pucca	70	42	112 (8.81%)
Total	**746 (58.65%)**	**526 (41.36%)**	**1272 (100%)**

As the above table 05.04 reveals that 87.58% of the Tribal Women live in kachcha house. Out of the total population 8.81% respondents live in semi pucca house and 3.62% respondents live in pucca house made of cement and bricks. An analysis of the type of dwelling house reveals that most of the respondents are drawn from economically lower status group. Thus, this table reveals that there is positive co-relationship in economic status of the respondents.

Pattern of Housing (Ownership)

One of the basic necessities of human life is a house to live in. Ownership of such necessities gives a psychological satisfaction. It also reflects the economic status and living standard of the people. Tribal living in village have, by and large, their own houses and very few live in rented accommodation. The housing pattern in villages is generally a reflection of social status by caste. Therefore, people belonging to a particular community, generally, reside in a particular area of the village.

Table : 05.05

Distribution of the Tribal Women Living as Tenant

Response	Chiniya	Bhandariya	Total
Yes	6	10	16 (1.26%)
No	740	516	1256
Total	746	526	1272

On the basis of above table 05.05, it shows that out of total respondents only 1.26%respondents are living as tenent, whereas majority of respondents with 98.75% have their own house for living.

Number of Rooms in The House of the respondents

The economic and social status of a family is measured by the number of rooms in the house in which it lives. The tribal's concept of a house is different from that of urban understanding. Most of the tribals have only one room in the house which is used for all purposes – cooking, living and sleeping. Those tribal families who are economically better off are having houses with multiple rooms. When describe the type of dwelling house it is important to know that in the houses of the

114

respondents how many rooms they have. As it is considered that no. of rooms describe the space for an individual in her house. As every human being need privacy. So it was asked to respondents that whether they have separate room for every one. The following table shows the no. of rooms in dwelling houses of the respondents.

Table : 05.06

No. of Rooms in the House of Tribal Women

No. of Rooms in house	Chiniya	Bhandariya	Total
1-2	266	328	594 (46.70%)
3-4	342	142	484 (38.06%)
5-6	98	34	132 (10.38%)
7-8 and above	40	22	62 (4.88%)
Total	746 (58.65%)	526 (41.36%)	1272 (100%)

As above table 05.06 reveals that while 46.70% respondents have only 1-2 rooms in their house, 38.06% respondents have 3-4 rooms in their house and 10.38% of respondents have 5-6 rooms in their house. Only 4.88% respondents have 7-8 and above rooms in their house. Thus, it is clear from the data that economic status has co-relationship with rooms in the house.

Place for kitchen

A woman spends more than half of the day in her kitchen. For the purpose of this study it was asked to respondents whether she has a separate place for kitchen in her house, as it signifies the major role of women as a home maker. The following table shows the separate place for kitchen in house.

115

Table : 05.07

Distribution on the basis of Separate Place for Kitchen in house

Separate kitchen in house	Chiniya	Bhandariya	Total
Yes	180	78	258 (20.29%)
No	566	448	1014 (79.72%)
Total	746 (58.65%)	526 (41.36%)	1272 (100%)

The above table 05.07 reveals that 79.72% respondents have no separate place for kitchen in their house. Only 20.29% respondents have separate place for kitchen in their house. The analysis of this table is that there is no scope for women to show her individual importance as a home maker. They have lesser status in their house. Ninety percent of the Indian household uses firewood, cow dung and crop residues as fuel. Burning of these fuels produce highly carbonated smoke: continuous respiration of which causes or help to cause many fatal diseases including cancer. The effects of inhalation of smoke are many. Evidence of heart disease called 'pulmonate' has been traced in persons who are exposed to smoke/inhale smoke, which has been found in cigarette smokers only. Studies in the northern part of India and Nepal indicated that persons exposed to such pollution are susceptible to chronic bronchitis. it also has an adverse effect on children and infants. One of the main reasons for the high morbidity and mortality rate in infants were found to be acute respiratory infection. It is partially due to irritation caused by such indoor, smoke filled conditions, in the rural areas and urban slums (Shah Giri Raj, 2008 p. 807-08).

Distribution on the basis of uses of Utensils in house

Items	Chiniya	Bhandariya	Total
Clay	18	-	18 (0.91%)
Aluminium	408	348	756 (38.03%)
Copper	-	-	-
Brass	-	-	-
Bronze	4	22	26 (1.31%)
Iron	-	-	-
Steel	694	494	1188 (59.76%)
Total	1124 (56.54%)	864 (43.47%)	1988 (100%)

The above table 05.08 reveals that the total population use various kinds of utensils made of many metals 59.76% respondents told that they use the utensils made of steel for cooking and serving food. 38.03% respondents use aluminium and 1.31% and 0.91% respondents use clay and bronze respectively. This fact shows that due to contact of new technologies and urban market, now the tribal are trying to use utensils of various types in place of clay.

Table : 05.09

Distribution on the basis of Availability of Toilets

Types of Toilets	Chiniya		Bhandariya		Total
	Yes	No	Yes	No	
Dry toilets	2	2	-	2	6 (0.48%)
Outside in agri. farms	-	-	-	2	2 (0.16%)
Payakhana	4	738	10	512	1264 (99.38%)
Total	6 (0.81%)	740 (99.20%)	10 (1.91%)	516 (98.10%)	1272 (100%)

On the basis of above table no. 05.09, it is clear from the fact about the types of toilets in the house. When it was asked to respondents whether they have toilets facility in their house, 99.20% respondents answered in negative. Only 0.81% respondents said they have dry toilets and paykhana in their home in Chiniya block. In Bhandariya block 98.10% respondents said they do not have any kind of toilets facility at their home. Only 1.91% respondents answered that they have payakhana at their home. In the research study it was observed that there were no private or public latrines and the tribal women had to go to their fields instead. The children often used the lanes and streets of village for this purpose. During monsoon days, when the sowing was over and field were pregnant with the crop, even the elders did not hesitate to use any place as their latrines.

Therefore, this resulted into the health related problems of respondents. Women go toilets early in the morning, before family member get up and start their daily life because in day time it is embarrassing for women to go for toilets in front of other members in the family. This is important to consider that women are still not getting safe and clean toilets facilities in the rural areas.

Table : 05.10

Distribution on the basis of Arrangement of Lights in house

Types of Lighting	Chiniya	Bhandariya	Total
Electric	2	10	12 (0.94%)
Karosin oil	744	526	1270 (99.07%)
Gas	-	-	-
Others	-	-	-
Total	746 (58.2%)	536 (41.81%)	1282 (100%)

As the above table no. 05.10 depicts that when it was asked to respondents about kind of arrangement for lighting in the night they have in their house. Out of the total population 99.07% respondents told that they use kerosene for lighting the lamps in the night. 0.94% respondents said they have electricity connection in their house.

Therefore, it is important to consider that those who have high economic status they have electricity in their house. Whereas those who belong to low economic group dependent on kerosene for light in their house. This results into domestic pollution in houses. which cause various breathing difficulties. Another fact is that there is a need of electricity connection in remote areas of the district and in dense forest areas: where most of the respondents are residing.

Table : 05.11

Distribution on the basis of Fuel Consumption in house

Items	Chiniya	Bhandariya	Total
Wood	720	518	1238 (95.53%)
Scrap from lands	4	26	30 (2.32%)
Cow Dung cake	-	2	2 (0.16%)
Coal	-	-	-
Karosin oil	-	-	-
Others	22	4	26 (2.01%)
Total	746 (57.57%)	550 (42.44%)	1296 (100%)

The table no 05.11 depicts that out of the total population, 95.53% respondents used fuel wood as for cooking and to keep their house warm in winter season. 2.32% respondents use residues or scraps they collected from the forest. 0.16% respondents use cow dung cakes as fuel for cooking. Only 2.01% respondents use other types of fuel.

Farm expenditure

It has been observed that agriculture is dominant in tribal economy of selected study. As such farm expenditure is very high. In farm expenditure include expenses on fertilizers, seeds, irrigation cost, labour charge etc. The following table shows the annual expenditure of respondents on an average. The items of expenditure are enumerated against each item the total expenditure incurred by the respondents is given below with the percentage.

Table : 05.12

Distribution on the basis of farm expenditure

Items	Chiniya		Bhandariya		Total	%
	No. of Respondents	Average / Annual ex.	No. of Respondents	Average / Annual ex.		
Ploughing	244	2550(30600)	103	2550 (30600)	61200	18.27
Agriculture instruments	333	1025 (12300)	102	1125 (13500)	25800	7.70
Manure	352	3050 (36600)	104	3550 (42600)	79200	23.65
Seeds	348	3050 (36600)	101	550 (6600)	43200	12.90
Labour charges	83	2550 (30600)	4	3250 (39000)	112800	33.69
Others	19	1050 (12600)	0	0	12600	3.76
Total	1379	13275 (159300)	414	11025 (132300)	334800	100

As table No. 05.12 shows that over ploughing of the respondents were spent a sum of Rs. 61200 with the percentage of 18.27. For purchasing of agricultural instruments, tribal women spent a sum of Rs. 25800 of total annum expenditure with the percentage of 7.70. Out of the total population for the purchasing of manure, respondents spent a sum of Rs. 79200 with the percentage of 23.65. For the purchasing of seeds respondents spent a sum of Rs. 43200 with the percentage of 12.90. Out of the total population respondents spent total amount of expenditure on

120

labour charges with the percentage of 33.69. Expenditure over other items are very negligible number 12600 with the percentage of 3.76. Therefore, it is clear from the above figure that respondents under the various categories spent so much money related to agricultural work.

Table : 05.13

Distribution of Satisfaction from Agriculture

Response	Chiniya	Bhandariya	Total
Yes	76	40	116 (9.12%)
No	670	486	1156 (90.89%)
Total	746 (58.65%)	526 (41.36%)	1272 (100%)

On the basis of above Table 05.13, out of the total population 1272, 90.89% respondents are not satisfied with their agriculture work which is major indicator of economic status of tribal women. Only 9.12% respondents are satisfied with their agriculture work.

Table : 05.14

Distribution on the basis of Sources of Irrigation

Sources	Chiniya	Bhandariya	Total
Rain	598	474	1072(57.95%)
Pond	170	120	290 (15.68%)
Well	314	48	362(19.57%)
Pumping set	48	6	54 (2.92%)
Others	64	8	72 (3.9%)
Total	1194 (64.55%)	656 (35.55%)	1850 (100%)

The above table no 05.14 shows that sources of irrigation around 57.95% respondents of the total population informed that they are solely dependents on the rain. 15.68% respondents depend on natural ponds. 19.57% respondents use the well for irrigation and 2.92% and 3.9% respondents are using pumping set and others sources of irrigation respectively. It is also observed that many hand pumps which were provided, are not functional in some villages. They were not maintained properly and ultimately the tribals again had to resort to other sources of water like ponds, streams for drinking and other purposes for which they have to travel a long distance. These sources of water are not safe for drinking purpose and are contaminated.

Table : 05.15

Distribution on the basis of Collection of Forest Produce or Residues

Produced (Goods)	Chiniya	Bhandariya	Total
Mahoua	718	492	1210 (56.65%)
shahtute	10	2	12 (0.57%)
Chiraungi (Piyar)	430	362	792 (37.08%)
Bair	32	54	86 (4.03%)
Others	26	10	36 (1.69%)
Total	1216 (56.93%)	920 (43.08%)	2136 (100%)

The above table no. 05.15 shows revealing that out of the total population 56.65% respondents collect mahua for additional source of income 37.08% respondents collect the piyar and chiraungi 4.03% respondents collect bair from the forest and 1.69% and 0.57% respondents collect forest produce and shahtute respectively.

Table : 05.16

Distribution on the basis of after Selling the Forest produces

Response	Chiniya	Bhandariya	Total
Yes	670	206	876 (68.87%)
No	76	320	396 (31.14%)
Total	746 (58.65%)	526 (41.36%)	1272 (100%)

On the basis of above table, 05.16 out of the total population, 68% respondents reported that they sell all the forest produce or residue for additional income. 31.14% respondents revealed that they do not sell forest produce as they use it for their own sake.

The Animals and Birds Domesticated by the Tribal Women

The breeding of cattle has always played an important role in tribals economy. Plough bullocks are indispensable to the cultivator and cow are kept much more for the sake of the bull calves they produce than for dairy purposes. Though tribals do milk their cows, milk is not an essential item in their diet. But in the olden days when land was not privately owned, cattle were the main symbol of wealth as the myths and epics tell of the vast herds of cattle owned by tribes.

Cattle are normally kept in pens or sheds throughout the night and taken to pasture during the day. Most of the cattle sheds and pens lie on the out skirts of the midst of plots used for vegetables and for such crops as need regular maturing. Some sheds are built and thatched like houses, but many people keep their cattle throughout the year in open pens walled with bamboo stockades. Plough bullocks are usually kept in separate sheds which are often situated inside the village. Many tribes voice the opinion that in their childhood there were larger herds of cattle than nowadays. The breeding of cattle for sale has assumed a role of some important in tribal economy (Sahay. k. k., 2005.82).

Like the other castes and tribes of the region, the tribes too domesticate animals which are helpful to them in their economic life.

Table : 05.17

Animals and birds owned by the Tribal Women

Animals /	Chiniya	Bhandariya	Total
Cow	332	140	472
Ox	558	330	888
Goat	582	290	872
Sheep	378	172	550

Pigs	62	114	176
Hen	2	6	8 (0.26%)
Duck	46	10	56 (1.77%)
Others	20	-	20 (0.63%)
Nothing	28	110	138
Total	**2008(63.15%)**	**1172(36.86%)**	**3180 (100%)**

Note: Total number of animals is shown in the table as respondents had more than one animal. So, total number exceeds the actual number of respondents.

On the basis of above table 05.17, the total 3180 animals and birds are domesticated by the respondents 27.93% domesticated ox for farming, 27.43% respondents domesticated goat for milk and after they sell out goats for other income also.14.85% respondents domesticated cows for milk and for her dung for fuel consumption.5.54%respondents have pigs. 1.77%respondents domesticated duck for flash and eggs.0.63% respondents have other animals for domestication whereas 4.34% respondents do not have any kind of animals for domestication.

Family Expenditure

The expenditure pattern of a society reflects the pattern and status of the society in general and individual in particular along with other information detailed information have been collected on items and amounts of expenditure. Most of the information has been collected for the whole year like, fuel, clothing, festivals, house maintenance, medicine etc. For food items average monthly expenditure have been recorded.

In expenditure, major share has been consumed by food items which is very obvious in rural and lower middle class societies.

Table : 05.18

Distribution on the basis of monthly expenses in the family

Items	Chiniya		Bhandariya		Total	%
	No. of Respondents	Average / Monthly ex.	No. of Respondents	Average / Annual		
Food	366	4550	106	4200	8750	41.10
Cloths	305	4025	105	1520	5545	26.05
Education	263	1510	55	360	1870	8.78
Medicine	329	525	104	525	1050	4.93
Fuel	213	260	96	275	535	2.51
Festival	155	525	82	525	1050	4.93
Addiction	321	255	89	260	515	2.41
Recreation	82	110	14	525	635	2.98
Cosmetics	227	255	27	255	510	2.39
Causal	24	525	14	300	825	3.87
Total	**2285**	**12540**	**692**	**8745**	**21285**	**100**

On the basis of above table 05.18, it was observed that all the items of expenditure are necessary for monthly basis, for food of the respondents spend sum of total amount 8750Rs. with 41.10%.for purpose of cloths sum of total amount was 5545 with 26.05%.for the purpose of education sum of total amount were 1870 with 8.78%. for the purpose of medical need 4.93% with sum total of 1050. for the purpose of festivals celebrations, for the expenses on addiction of liquor the respondents spend total sum of Rs.515 with 2.41%.cosmatics and casual expenses was done by respondents with total sum of 510 and 825 Rs. with 2.39 and3.87%respectivly.

Indebtedness

The concept of loan has changed with time. The old saying neither a debtor nor a lender be may at time took very ideal but it is difficult to adhere to it. In developing economy, loan is a part of budget for the state. This aspect is equally good for an individual. Due to lack of saving the agriculturists, traders and other people need some credit for capital. These types of loan are useful as they help in boosting the economy. But side by side the tribals incur inevitable loan to meet their basic necessities and many times to meet the expenses of social and religious ceremonies. So far the individual family, is concerned the loan is a complex phenomenon, a blending of consumption and capital credits (sahay., 2005.79).

Table : 05.19

Distribution of the Tribal Women of Borrowing Money by family

Response	Chiniya	Bhandariya	Total
Yes	190	108	298 (23.43%)
No	556	418	974 (32.87%)
Total	746 (58.65%)	526 (41.36%)	1272 (100%)

As the above table 05.19 shows that the amount borrowed by the 298 respondents out of 1272 households is represented in above mentioned table. While 23.43% respondents have borrowed money from different source. 32.87% respondents have not taken money as loan.

Table : 05.20

Distribution on the basis of borrowing money individually

Response	Chiniya	Bhandariya	Total
Yes	492	86	578 (45.44%)
No	254	440	694 (54.55%)
Total	746	526	1272 (100%)

On the basis of above table 05.20, while out of the total respondents,54.55% not borrowed money for individual purposes only 45.44% respondents have taken money as loan for individual reasons.

Purpose of Loan

It has been experienced that in rural tribal areas the beneficiaries of institutional financing have taken loan mostly for productive purposes but uses the same for consumption and social needs. Thus there is always a difference in useful need and utilization. Different lead Banks and Gramin Banks of the districts have their district credit plans (D.C.P.). The financing in the area are estimated with certain goals and the estimated credit requirement is apportioned to different bank and credit institutions working for extending loan are agriculture and business etc. this is obvious according to rural credit policies.

The credit trend as have been reflected by the loans taken shows that agriculture sector is the prime consumer of loans. Together with irrigation and other inputs the total agriculture sector has covered as much as 54% of the total loan (Sahay, 2005.80).

Table : 05.21

Distribution on the basis of reasons borrowing money

Purpose of taking loan	Chiniya		Bhandariya		Total	%
	No. of Respondents	Amount in Rs.	No. of Respondents	Amount in Rs.	Total of amont Rs.	
For farming	118	5050	15	5250	10433	20.39
For marriage	43	4100	8	3500	7651	14.95
For education	34	1600	7	1050	2691	5.26
For medicine	145	4050	23	1950	6168	12.05
For religion	12	2600	6	1100	3718	7.26
After crops not Produce	7	2600	0	0	2607	5.09
For purchasing	59	12650	18	5150	17877	34.95
Total	418	32650	77	18000	51145	100

The above table 05.21 shows that amount borrowed by the 418 of Chiniya block, 77 by the respondents of Bhandariya block respectively on the basis of above table for farming purpose, the respondents borrowed a sum of Rs. 10433 with 20.39% for the purpose of marriage, respondents borrowed a sum of Rs. 7651 with 14.95%. For the purpose of education respondents borrowed a sum of Rs. 2691Rs. with 5.26%. For the purpose of medicines, the respondents borrowed a sum of Rs. 6168 with 12.05%. For the purpose of religious activities, respondents borrowed a sum of Rs. 3718 with 7.26% the respondents borrowed money after non-production of crops in farm with sum of 5.09%. For the purpose of purchasing animals, the respondents borrowed money sum of Rs. 17877 with 34.95%. Therefore it is clear from the facts that major reason for purpose of loan were for purchasing animals.

Goods Utility of Tribal Women

House hold articles, dress and ornaments in tribes are an index of tremendous change. This is due to two main reasons viz ailability of such articles in the tribal market (local haat) and contact with other neighbours who are mostly people of Hindu community and local tribes. Tribal women try to imitate household articles, dress and ornaments of their neighbours.

Table : 05.22

Garments wear by the Tribal Women

Garments	Chiniya	Bhandariya	Total
Sarees	746	526	1272 (98.3%)
Salwar – suit	10	8	18 (1.4%)
Gown (maxi)	2	2	4 (0.31%)
lehanga	-	-	-
Others	-	-	-
Total	**758 (58.58%)**	**536 (41.43%)**	**1294 (100%)**

On the basis of above table 05.22 out of the total population, while 98.3% respondents wear only sarees, 1.4% and 0.31% respondents wear salwar-suit and gown (maxi) respectively. In this connection it is important to know that what kind of texture or clothes. they use to wear. The above table shows the kind of clothes respondents use to wear.

Table : 05.23

Type of cloths utilised by the Tribal Women

Cloths	Chiniya	Bhandariya	Total
Cotton	604	104	708 (41.26%)
Polyesters	220	164	384 (22.38%)
Tricot	294	330	624 (36.37%)
Others	-	-	-
Total	**1118 (65.16%)**	**598 (34.85%)**	**1716 (100%)**

On the basis of above table 05.23 the fact revealed that out of the total population 41.26% respondents use cotton, 22.38% respondents use polyester clothes and 36.37% respondents use tricot clothes. On the basis of above facts it is important to know that frequency of purchasing garments in a year is shown in the following table.

Table : 05.24

Yearly purchasing of cloths by the Tribal Women

No. of clothes	Chiniya	Bhandariya	Total
1	400	284	684 (53.53%)
2	320	210	530 (41.48%)
3	32	32	64 (5.08%)
Others	-	-	-
Total	752 (58.85%)	526 (41.16%)	1278 (100%)

The above table 05.24 reveals that 53.53% respondents purchase only one garment in a year. While 41.48% respondents said that they purchase two garments in a year, only 5.08% respondents purchase three garments in a year.

Table : 05.25

Items of luxury owned by the Tribal Women

Items	Chiniya	bhandariya	total
Radio	56	30	86 (2.63%)
Colour T. V.	2	6	8 (0.25%)
Cooker	0	2	2 (0.07%)
Watch	82	122	204 (6.24%)
Table	28	18	46 (1.41%)
Repicot	648	512	1160
Choki	538	196	734 (22.44%)
Chair	370	146	516 (15.78%)
Water pump	26	10	36 (1.11%)

Handpump	14	4	18 (0.56%)
Machine	4	6	10 (0.31%)
Telephone	10	2	12 (0.37%)
Mobile	218	96	314 (9.6%)
Gadda	4	2	6 (0.19%)
Chulha	16	8	24 (0.74%)
Nothing	92	4	96 (2.94%)
Total	**2108**	**1164**	**3272 (100%)**

Note: Total number of items is shown in the table as respondents had more than one luxury items. So, total member exceeds the actual number of respondents and so percentage has been taken of each item.

On the basis of table no 05.25 out of the total number of 3272 articles possessed by all respondent, 2.94% (96) respondents do not have any item of luxury, it is found that mobiles are prominent in rural areas. There are 9.6% (314) respondents have who mobile phone. When it was asked to the respondents about possession of cots, choki, chair, 35.46% (1160) respondents said that they have cot, 22.44% (734), 15.78% (516) respondents have choki and chairs respectively and 2.63% (86) respondents have radios in their houses.

Although, they do not have many articles of luxury there is a clear indication of the fact that, they are conscious of the importance of the mass media and that, they are bent upon having articles of luxuries when their financial position improves. There are 15.78% (516) chairs: some of them are wooden and some other are of iron. There are only 1.41% (46) tables which means respondents have the habit of writing or they use it for keeping things which cannot be put on the floor.

So the respondents have vehicles and articles of luxury in low percentage. Among articles include table, choki, chair, and cot which are predominant as these are necessary for their life or rest. So their material culture holds mirror not only to their economic condition but also to the fact that their outlook towards material culture is also changing.

REFERENCES

> Choudhary, D.S.   (1981) :'Emerging Rural Leadership in An Indian State',
Manthan Publication, New Delhi, p. 56.

> Dharshankar,   (1979) :'Leadership in Panchayat Raj', Panchsheel Prakashan,
Jaipur, pp. 89-90.

> Dharshankar, A. Y.,   (1979) :'Leadership in Panchayati Raj', Panchsheel Prakashan,
Jaipur, p. 90.

> Giri, Raj. Saha   (2008) :'The encyclopaedia of women's studies', vol-2. gyan
Publishing house, New Delhi p-807.

> Harsurkar R. Laxmi   (2005) :'the tribes and their development', Current
Publication., Agra. p80.

> Kalgi, B. B.,   (2008) :'The scheduled tribes in transition', Classical
Publishing company. New Delhi. P-120.

> Karlo, Rejir.   (2005) :'Emerging pattern of tribal leadership in arunachal
Pradesh', Common wealth New Delhi. p47.

> Sahay, K. K.,   (2005) :'Development of goand tribes in modern perspective',
Classical Publishing Company. New Delhi, p.135.

> Sikligar, P. C.   (2006) :'Empowerment of tribal women wavli', Mangal deep
Publications Jaipur., p-92.

CHAPTER – IV

WORK LOAD AND GENDER DISCRIMINATION, EXPLOITATION OF TRIBAL WOMEN

Table : 06.01

Distribution on the basis of the working in MGNREGA

Response	Chiniya	Bhandariya	Total
Yes	540	318	858 (67.46%)
No	206	208	414 (32.55%)
Total	746 (58.65%)	526 (41.36%)	1272 (100%)

On the basis of above table 06.01, it is clear that out of the total population 67.46% respondents were working as a labour under the MGNREGA.32.55% respondents told that they are not working as a labour under MGNREGA.

Table : 06.02

Distribution on the basis of getting money (salary) timely

Response	Chiniya	Bhandariya	Total
Yes	394	174	568 (44.66%)
No	352	352	704 (55.35%)
Total	746(58.65%)	526 (41.36%)	1272 (100%)

Table No. 06.02 narrates that when it was asked to respondents whether they get timely payment of their job 44.66% respondents reported that they get timely payment when they go for work outside the village. 55.35% respondents told that they do not get timely payment of their job or work.

Table : 06.03

Distribution on the basis of getting full payment in MGNREGA

Response	Chiniya	Bhandariya	Total
Yes	466	182	648 (50.95%)
No	280	344	624 (49.06%)
Total	746 (58.65%)	526 (41.36%)	1272 (100%)

Table 06.03 narrates that when respondents were asked about whether they are getting full payment under MGNREGA. Scheme to know the economic exploitation of respondents being a female; women get less payment than men. In this regard while 50.95% respondents replied in positive that they get full payment under MGNREGA, only 49.06% respondents reported in negative that they do not get full payment under MGNREGA.

The table 06.04 shows the ability of the respondents to save and also the extent of their savings. The earning capacity of the households under study is limited on account of so many factors, such as exclusive dependent upon caste occupation or traditional occupation and very narrow margin of saving and so on.

Table : 06.04

Distribution on the basis of saving money

Response	Chiniya	Bhandariya	Total
Yes	398	128	526 (41.36%)
No	348	398	746 (58.65%)
Total	746 (58.65%)	526 (41.36%)	1272 (100%)

On the basis of above table 06.04 out of the total population only 41.36% respondents were able to save money. 58.65% respondents reported that they were not able to save money since they spend a lot of money in drinking, especially, on the occasions of festivals and functions.

Saving is common with the female members of the selected blocks. They contribute, considerable amount to the income by their diligence and hard work. So they are bent on saving as much as possible.

Role of Tribal Women in household Work

Women are primarily responsible for the health, nutrition, hygiene level and comfort of their families. Women play an important role in tribal economy. Apart from their domestic work, women used to attend work to help husbands in construction and repair of houses as unskilled worker. Agriculture and casual labourer women in fact work hard and perform dual role in the domestic and productive role along with childbearing and child-rearing. They work even before the delivery and start working again after 2-3 days of delivery. It means they hardily take rest and appropriate nutrition after the delivery, which is generally preferred by women of other society (Sikligar, P.C. 2006 P. 43)

Table : 06.05

Distribution on the basis of role of female in house hold work

Daily house hold work	Chiniya		Bhandariya	
	Yes	No	Yes	Total of y. (%)
Child rearing	426	320	32	458 (19.34)
Cooking food	418	328	30	448 (18.91)
Washing cloths	408	338	30	438 (18.49)
Cutting woods	346	400	14	360 (15.20)
Dusting	368	378	24	392 (16.55)
Caring of animals	176	570	14	190 (8.02)
Caring of elders	38	708	10	48 (2.02)
Shopping	30	716	4	34 (1.43)
Total				**2368 (100)**

On the basis of above table 4.6 an average of total respondents have been taken to shows that in given household work of respondents, every respondent does seven to eight work in daily households chores. 19.34% respondents do child rearing, 18.91% respondents do cooking, 18.49% respondents wash clothes, 15.20% respondents cut woods for fuel, 16.55% respondents do dusting in their house, 8.02% respondents care their animals, only 2.02% and 1.43% respondents take care of elders and shopping respectively.

Migration of Tribal Women

A large number of women and girls from tribal areas migrate to cities and towns all over India. Most of these women and girls are illiterate and unskilled. They work in inhuman conditions in cities as their living standard is extremely poor A great number of these migrants are subjected to exploitation by middlemen, contractors and employers. Many of these women and girls work as house maids where their working hours extend up to 18 hours a day. A large number of tribal women and girls become victims of sexual and financial exploitation. Their children rarely get an opportunity to go to school and learn a productive skill. Gradually many women and girls lose contact with their kith and kins and become alienated from their culture and roots.

Table : 06.05

Distribution on the basis of work done by Tribal Women besides farming

Reasons	Chiniya	Bhandariya	Total
Migrated to other cities	300	252	552 (43.33%)
Work as a domestic servant	8	18	26 (2.05%)
Traditional jobs (basket & hand fans making)	76	92	168 (13.19%)
Dependents on others income	68	108	176 (13.82%)
Others	296	56	352 (27.63%)
Total	**748 (58.72%)**	**526 (41.29%)**	**1274 (100%)**

On the basis of above table no. 06.05, it is also seen that agriculture and agricultural labour and their allied activities are the main occupation of tribes of Garhwa district. In addition to these main occupations they carry on many other activities to supplement their income. They are their secondary occupations. An attempt is made to describe their various secondary occupations which are also important for their income.

The respondents revealed the fact they migrated to other regions or other state in search of job, when there is no season of cultivation or sometimes they are forced to do other job due to their low economic status and to get additional money for survival.

Out of the total population 43.33% (552) respondents migrated to other cities or states. 13.19% (168) respondents reported that they do their traditional job for instances, basket making, net making, pot making and others. 13.82% (176) respondents reported that they depend on other members of the family. 27.63% (352) respondents reported that they do some secondary job, when they are not engaged in the agricultural fields. Only 2.05% (26) respondents reported that they work as a servant in other houses or in the home of rich people or those people who have high economic status.

Table : 06.06

Distribution on the basis of Female members in family

Female member	Chiniya	Bhandariya	Total
Girls	1380	820	2200 (59.76%)
Adults	552	546	1098 (29.83%)
Olds	296	88	384 (10.43%)
Total	**2228 (60.52%)**	**1454 (39.49%)**	**3682 (100%)**

On the basis of above table number of female population in selected household while 59.76% females were found girls, 29.83% females were adults, Only 10.43% females were aged women.

Table : 06.07 and 6.8

In tribal society girls child does not face any bias like in Hindu social system. Most of the tribal girls follow certain characteristics like obedient, hardworking, good character, respect elders, humble etc. Tribal girls even in young age go for work and the income earned by them is handed over to the family. Tribal girls should help mother in her chores as well as she should not become shirker so that others may not make comment on mother that she has not made her perfect in work.

Distribution on the basis of work done by boys and girls

Work done by boys / girls	Chiniya Bhandariya				Girls boys		Total
	Girls/boys		Boys/Girl				
	Yes	Yes	Yes	Yes	yes	yes	
House hold work	1186	1384	632	628	1818	2012	3830(22.7%)
Farming (Agriculture work)	1144	1230	302	336	1446	1532	3012(34.54%)
To bring fuel from Forest	450	442	182	120	632	562	1194(13.69%)
Working as a servant in other home	50	102	46	36	116	136	234(2.68)
Work as a shepherd	112	276	8	32	120	308	428(4.90)
others	10	12	-	-	10	12	22(0.25)
Total							8720(100)

In the above table no. 06.07 and 06.08 households responsibilities which is shared by both boys and girls in the family. Total sum of the responses taken by calculating an average of each household duties 22.7% both boys and girls do house hold work, 34.54% boys and girls help parents in farming, 13.69% girls and boys bring fuel from forest for cooking food, 2.68% respondents shared that they work as a servant in others home as a servant or care taker, 4.90% boys and girls work as shepherd. Very few respondents do other work for family.

Table : 06.09 and 06.10

Distribution on the basis of children going to school

Block /	Boys		Girls		Total
	Yes	No	Yes	No	
Chiniya	1308	178	1174	206	2866(62.87%)
Bhandariya	608	264	570	250	1692(37.12%)
Total	**1916**	**442**	**1744**	**456**	**4558(100%)**

With reference to know that respondents are sending their children (boys & girls) to school. Out of 4558 population of children, 62.87% children go to school for study. Only 37.12% children do not go to school for study. There were various reasons why children are not going to school?

Distribution on the basis of children not going to school

Reasons	Chiniya		Bhandariya		Total
	Boys	Girl	Boys	Girl	
Don't know	36	35	83	124	278(30.95%)
Responsibility of younger siblings	36	62	80	42	220(24.49%)
House-hold Responsibility	17	52	35	20	124(13.80%)
manual labour	20	15		10	45(6.12%)
Study is not necessary	13	8	15	12	48(5.34%)
So expensive			20	35	55(6.12%)
Not interested in study	38		10		48(5.34%)
No facilities in school for	18	9	12	7	46(5.12%)
Due to marriage		11	9		20(2.22%)
Others		14			14(1.55%)
Total	**178**	**206**	**264**	**250**	**898(100%)**

Out of 898 children, 30.95% respondents said that they do not know the reasons. May be they were conscious to hesitate to answer it. 24.49% respondents said their children have responsibilities of younger siblings as they help mother to care younger. 13.80% children shoulders household responsibilities of their mother,

138

5.1% children go for labouring. 5.34% said study is not necessary. 6.02% said study is so expensive that their parents cannot afford. 5.34% have no interest in study. 5.12% girls do not have facility for school. Negligible numbers of children had not gone to school due to marriage (2.22%) and others reasons 1.55% respectively.

Domestic violence includes not only inter spousal violence but also violence perpetrated by other family members. Generally an important part of the power relationship between spouses and their families relates to dowry and its ramifications.

Domestic violence has been defined as all actions by the family against one of its members that threaten the life, body, psychological integrity or liberty of the members. The forms of violence commonly found were slapping, kicking, tearing hair, pushing and pulling, hitting with an object, attempting to strangulate and threatening. Forms of psychological abuse were also found to exist, for instance, verbal abuse, sarcastic remarks in the presence of outsiders, imposing restrictions on freedom of movement, totally ignoring the wife in decision making process, making frequent complaints against her to her parents, friend, neighbours and kin much to the embarrassment of the wife. Some of the reasons given by the women were financial matters, behaviour with in laws, back biting, talking to any male without the liking of the husband, asking for money, preventing him from drinking and husbands personality traits.

Table : 06.11

Have you ever fight with husband

Response	Chiniya	Bhandariya	Total
Yes	460	254	714 (56.14%)
No	286	272	558 (43.87%)
Total	**746 (58.65%)**	**526 (41.36%)**	**1272 (100%)**

On the basis of above table no. 06.11 the major facts has come up that out of the total respondents while 56.14% revealed that they fight with their husband, 43.87% respondents replied they do not fight with their husband.

Table : 06.12

Have you been beaten by your husband

Response	Chiniya	Bhandariya	Total
Yes	214	136	350 (27.52%)
No	532	390	922 (72.49%)
Total	746 (58.65%)	526 (41.36%)	1272 (100%)
If yes, 5.8-1 Reasons	y-214	y -136	
Due to Alcoholism	118	56	174 (49.72%)
Suspicious nature	42	38	80 (22.86%)
Not able to do House hold work	30	20	50 (14.29%)
Interested in another woman	24	22	46 (13.15%)
Total	**214 (61.15%)**	**136 (38.86%)**	**350 (100%)**

In table no. 06.12 when it was asked to the respondents, majority of tribal women responded positively in addition, it was asked to respondents whether they have been ever beaten up by their husband. While 27.52% respondents told they have been beaten up by their husband, 72.49% respondents have not been beaten by their husband.

Besides this, respondents were also asked what are the major reasons of their fighting with husband. The various reasons throw light upon the relationship status of couples. 49.72% respondents told that habit of taking liquor of husband is the major reason. 22.86% respondents revealed that their husband suspect that she has extra marital relation with another man, 14.29% respondents revealed that family members think she is not able to do household work perfectly 13.15% tribal women think that their spouse has other women in his life.

Therefore, marital violence has been by and large a feature of family life among the tribals to which the society has usually turned a blind eye. Marital violence is symptomatic of the more general oppression of women in patriarchal society. Millions of women bear this quietly and silently. Researched reasons broadly appear to be alcoholism, poverty, psycho-sexual problem, immaturity, high expectations, and different level of tolerance (Shah: Raj Giri, 2008, P. 382).

Table : 06.13

Have you been misbehaved or touched by any male

Response	Chiniya	Bhandariya	Total
Yes	310	158	468 (36.8%)
No	436	368	804 (63.21%)
Total	746 (58.65%)	526 (41.36%)	1272 (100%)

In the above table respondents were asked whether they have been sexually harassed by any man in the form of touching or misbehave. While 36.8% respondents told that they have sexually harassed by another man, 63.21% respondents replied in negative.

141

Table : 06.14

Did you not like any talk or incident by any male

Response	Chiniya	Bhandariya	Total
Yes	94	86	180 (14.16%)
No	652	440	1092 (85.85%)
Total	746 (58.65%)	526 (41.36%)	1272 (100%)
If yes, 6.14-1 Who,	Y-94	Y-86	
Family member	42	28	70 (38.89%)
Relatives	22	15	39 (20.56%)
Neighbours	18	35	53 (29.45%)
landlord / boss	12	8	20 (11.12%)
Total	**94 (52.23%)**	**86 (47.78%)**	**180 (100%)**

In the table no. 06.14, to know about the verbal violence or harassment, respondents were asked whether they have been victim of any verbal comment by any male. 85.85% respondents told that they did not face any verbal or non verbal behaviour by any male. Only 14.16% tribal women revealed that they faced verbal or non verbal behaviour by a male. Out of 180 (14.16%) respondents 38.89% respondents told it was done by family members. 29.45% complained that they had been neighbours had misbehaved. 20.56 and 11.12% women accepted that misbehaved by the relatives and landlord respectively.

Table : 06.15

Distributions on the basis of comments given by others

Person	Chiniya					Bhandariya					Total
	*1	*2	*	*	*	1	2	3	4	5	
Family member	25	17	-	-	-	-	-	-	15	13	70 (38.89%)
Relatives	-	10	-	-	12	-	-	-	-	15	39 (20.56%)
Neighbours	-	6	4	-	8	-	-	25	-	10	53 (29.45%)
landlord / boss	-	-	4	8	-	-	-	8	-		20 (11.12%)
Total	25 (13.89%)	33 (18.34%)	8 (4.45%)	8 (4.45%)	20 (11.12%)	-	-	33 (18.34%)	15 (8.34%)	38 (21.12%)	180 (100%)

* explanation of code

1 – She does not cook food properly 2 – She cannot deliver baby boy
3 – Making physical relation
4 – She does not do work properly 5 – This lady is witch

In relation to above mentioned table major reasons for verbal and nor-verbal categorised in five groups:

In Chiniya block, 13.89% respondents revealed that family member told that she can not cook food properly. 18.34% respondents said that family members, relatives, neighbour commented for she can not give birth boy. Of family members, relatives, neighbours, 4.45% respondents revealed that landlord and neighbour tried to make sexual relation with her, 4.45% women said that landlord commented that she cannot cook food properly. 11.12% respondents told that relative and neighbour alleged that she is a witch. With regard to Bhandaria block 18.34% women said that neighbour and landlord tried to sexually harassment. 8.34% women shared that family member commented or not do work properly. 21.12% women revealed that family members, relatives and neighbour has alleged she is a witch.

143

Any person tried to make physical relation for money

Response	Chiniya	Bhandariya	Total
Yes	348	102	450 (35.38%)
No	398	424	822 (64.63%)
Total	746 (58.65%)	526 (41.36%)	1272 (100%)

In the table no. 06.16. In further investigation when it was asked to respondents whether any person tried to make physical relations with her by giving money. With regard to this question 64.63% respondents replied that she has not been attempted by any male for physical relation. 35.38% respondents said they have been tried by male for making relation.

Table : 06.17

Distribution on the basis of Female paraded as nude

Response	Chiniya	Bhandariya	Total
Yes	38	12	50 (3.94%)
No	708	514	1222 (96.07%)
Total	746 (58.65%)	526 (41.36%)	1272 (100%)

With regard to table no. 06.17 even if having customary laws in the tribal community there are various incidents which throw light in the vulnerable condition of poor, illiterate, tribal women, some males or high status men by blaming a women characterless insulted her in front of all villagers to punish or teach a lesson for future. When it was asked to respondents whether any female has been paraded nude

144

in village recently, majority of respondents deny this fact with 96.07%. Only 3.94% respondents said it was happened in recent past.

Witch Crafting
Case study

Ilamma (60) belonged to a Scheduled Caste (Mala). She had a husband, a daughter and a son. The whole village (*Jukal* village, *Chityala* mandal, *Warangal* district in Telangana region) believed she was a sorcerer and held her responsible if the buffaloes stopped giving milk, or if children fell ill. In the year 2000, villagers boycotted her family. In due course, her daughter-in-law, also started projecting Ilamma as a sorcerer, probably because she felt the old woman was a heavy burden to feed, and held her responsible for her father's death. Ilamma left the village and went to her sister's place in *Bethikal* village, *Huzurabad* mandal, in *Karimnagar* district. After three years, one night in 2003, the villagers suspected that Ilamma had placed lemons before a few houses. The villagers, reportedly, searched Ilamma's house and found some lemons and turmeric powder in a bag. The furious villagers made her eat human excreta, they accused Ilamma of wandering around the village, at midnight, on *amavasya* and *pournami* days.

If the accusations of villagers were true, what could be the reasons behind her behaviour? She may be suffering from some mental illness. Who in the village could analyse and explain these things to the people? Is there any official in the village panchayat, hospital or revenue department who has some understanding of these things? Civil society and the government has the responsibility but they could not discharge the responsibility.

As of now, there is nobody to feed Ilamma. She can't toil. She is still alive like a living corpse with torn clothes and hunger in *Sirsapally* of *Huzurabad* mandal. So many Ilammas are being victimized by the negligent attitude of society. sill society's eyes remain closed.

In some cases, if women had properties in their names, their own family members projected those women as sorcerers and killed them. And in other instances, some dalit women were exploited and if some of them refused to yield, they were branded as sorcerers, paraded nude, and later killed. In one instance, one Dalit family head was killed in the name of practicing sorcery just because he refused to vote for a particular party.

Even the superstitions are used as oppressive methods against dalit women. There are several interconnected social, political and economic causes for the continued existence of these superstitions in the tribal societies.

Table : 06.18

Distributions on the basis of any woman killed as a witch

Response	Chiniya	Bhandariya	Total
Yes	102	70	172 (13.53%)
No	644	456	1100 (86.48%)
Total	746 (58.65%)	526 (41.36%)	1272 (100%)
If yes 6.18-1 Reasons	Y-102	Y-70	
Black Magic	24	25	49 (28.49%)
Make people sick	18	18	36 (20.94%)
Tortured family	45	11	56 (32.56%)
To make others scared/ afraid	15	16	31 (18.03%)
Total	**102 (59.31%)**	**70 (40.7%)**	**172 (100%)**

In relation to witch craft table no. 06.18 and 06.18.1, as it was discussed prior that in remote tribal area where police is unable to go to check the practice of witch crafting. Under this study when it was asked to respondents whether any woman was killed as a witch. Out of the total population 86.48% respondents derived this fact no one was killed branding as a witch. 13.53% respondents answered affirmatively that it was happened in their village. In addition to that respondents were asked that what were the major reasons for practising witch craft 28.49% stated that a woman was practising black magic in village. 20.94% respondents replied that woman was responsible for making villagers and family member sick or ill. 32.56% respondents said women who we called witch was harming family members. 18.03% respondents said that she used to make people scared in villages.

Table : 06.19

Any girl has been sold out

Response	Chiniya	Bhandariya	Total
Yes	150	18	168
No	596	508	1104
Total	**746**	**526**	**1272**

On the basis of above table no. 06.19, there was some cases came into focus of human trafficking in selected area of study. When it was asked to respondents whether any girl or woman was sold out in their knowledge. 86.8% respondents denied this fact, 13.21% respondents said they know that some girls have been sold out from their village.

Table 06.20

Any woman has been raped

Response	Chiniya	Bhandariya	Total
Yes	84	30	114 (8.97%)
No	662	496	1158
Total	**746**	**526**	**1272**

On the basis of table no. 06.20, rape is another offence of grave nature. Sexual intercourse with a married or unmarried girl without her consent is an offence. In tribal societies the rape has been committed by a man of other caste or tribe, the offender is beaten in presence of the panchayat officials of both sides. Under this study respondents said that such cases are seldom brought in the notice of the panchayat due to the shyness of the victim girl. In this regard, 91.04% respondents

147

denied that this was not happened in their village. Only 8.97% respondents said that it happened in their village recently.

Table : 06.21

Any girl has been eloped

Response	Chiniya	Bhandariya	Total
Yes	276	130	406 (31.91%)
No	470	396	866 (68.09%)
Total	**746 (58.65%)**	**526 (41.36%)**	**1272 (100%)**

On the basis of table no. 06.21, it was asked to respondents whether any woman or girl eloped by someone or villagers, while 68.09% respondents told there were no incident happened in their village. 31.91% respondents positively replied that girls have been eloped in their village.

REFERENCES

➢ Narayan, Kartik (2010)   : "Round the Table", Article.

➢ http//southasia.oneworld.net/fromthegrassroot

CHAPTER – VI
HEALTH RELATED MATTERS

Before studying the infrastructure, policy and measures of the Department of Health and Family Welfare, it is important to know the present state of health in the state. Jharkhand has a total population of 26.9 million of which 13.9 million were males and the remaining 13 million were females. For the period 1991-2001, Jharkhand's growth rate was much lower than that of its parent state of Bihar where it was 28.4%. But it was above national growth rate of 21.3% Inter-district variations are also significant. The growth rate in Garhwa and Chatra is 29% but as low as 16% in West Singhbhum and Gumla district. Another noteworthy feature is the marginal decrease in the population growth rate between 1981-1991 (24%) and between 1991-2001 (23.2%). However the growth rate in our state is higher than in many other states (Singh, sunil. 2004).

Table : 07.01

Distribution of the Tribal Women consultation taken when sick

Sources	Chiniya	Bhandariya	Total %
Govt.	154	60	214(14.90%)
Health camps	2	6	8(0.55%)
Ojha	34	218	252(17.54%)
N.G.O.	8	74	82(5.71%)
Quacks	554	326	880(61.285%)
Total	**752**	**684**	**1436 (100%)**

On the basis of above table no. 07.01 61.28% respondents take consultation from quacks (Jhola-chhap doctors) in sickness. 17.54% respondents take advice from Ojhas. 14.90% respondents take advice from government hospitals. Negligible number of respondents take advice from health camps (0.55%) and N.G.O s (5.71%) respectively. Women's health is also affected by their work. The relationship between work and health is quite complex. In addition, poverty, accessibility of hospitals at the time of delivery and acute or chronic disease are important factor of low health status of tribal women.

It is seen in the observation under study, tribal women still believe in the Ojha, Jholachhaap doctor or local treatment which worsens the condition of the health of tribal women. Inaccessibility to health care centres, absence of health staff, deplorable sanitary conditions in the health centres and lack of drugs are common factors which are responsible to low health status of tribal women. (Chaudhary, anita 2012 P. 104)

Malaria, T.B. like genital T.B. is one of the biggest killers of women in general and of women in the reproductive age group in particular. The transition from infection to the disease and its implication is rooted not merely in the biology but in the environment, social and material conditions of living. When women get infected, they are either sent back to their parental home for treatment or deserted. On the one hand, women find it difficult to travel to distant health centres or hospitals for diagnosis and treatment of T.B., as the treatment requires regular visits to health centres and, on the other hand, there is the absence of support system at home and financial help to meet the high cost of medicines. (Anita, 2012 P. 118)

Table : 07.02

Distribution of the Tribal Women having health problems

Response	Chiniya	Bhandariya	Total
Yes	372	128	500 (39.30%)
No	374	398	772 (60.69%)
Total	**746 (58.65%)**	**526 (41.36%)**	**1272 (100%)**
If yes, 7.2-1 (Disease)	**Y-372**	**Y-128**	
white discharge	138	30	168 (33.6%)
Back ache	18	12	30 (6%)

anaemic	8	-	8 (1.6%)
Burning feet	36	10	46 (9.2%)
Stomach ache	154	8	162 (32.4%)
Malaria	2	2	4 (0.8%)
Head ache	16	20	36 (7.2%)
Menstrual problem	-	26	26 (5.2%)
Diabetes	-	8	8 (1.6%)
Asthma	-	2	2 (0.4%)
Period problem	-	10	10 (2%)
Total	**372 (74.4%)**	**128 (25.6%)**	**500 (100%)**

In the table no. 07.02 when it was asked to respondents whether they have health related problems, 39.30% (500) respondents told that they have some health related problems whereas 60.69% respondents said they do not have any health problem. In addition, out of the 500 (39.30%) respondents, 33.6% women said they have white discharge (swet pradar), 32.4% respondents told they feel stomach-ache, 9.2% said they feel burning feet, 7.2% respondents told they have headache problem, 5.2% respondents have menstrual cycle problem, 6.0% respondents said they have back pain, only negligible number of respondents complained about asthma, diabetes, malaria, periodic problem of their health.

Table : 07.03

Distributions on the basis of pregnant Tribal Women

Response	Chiniya	Bhandariya	Total
Yes	218	40	258 (20.28%)
No	528	486	1014 (79.71%)
Total	**746 (58.65%)**	**526 (41.36%)**	**1272 (100%)**

In the table no. 07.03 with regard to know the status of pregnancy of respondents, 20.28% women told that they are pregnant. 79.71% respondents denied that they are pregnant.

Table : 07.04

Distributions on the basis of frequency of pregnancy

Frequency	Chiniya	Bhandariya	Total
0-1	116	274	390
2-4	340	154	494
5-6	206	60	266
7-8	78	36	114 (8.96%)
9-10	4	2	6 (0.47%)
11-12	2	-	2 (0.15%)
Total	746 (58.65%)	526 (41.36%)	1272 (100%)

Respondents were asked about their frequency of pregnancy to know, how many times they conceived. Out of the total population of understudy 30.66% revealed they got first time pregnancy, the class interval was adopted to know the frequency of pregnancy. 0-1, 2-4, 5-6, 7-8, 9-10, 11-12 times 38.83% respondents said they were 2 to 4 time pregnant, 20.91% respondents said they were pregnant about 5-6 times, 8.96% respondents told 7-8 times pregnant. Only 0.47% and 0.15% respondents said they were 9-10, 11-12 times pregnant respectively.

Nutritional Status of Women

Maternal malnutrition is a major cause of concern in Jharkhand. A little less than three-fourths of women suffer from anemia, a prevalence level much higher than the national average of 52%. About 30% suffer from moderate to severe anemia as compared with 17% of India as a whole. Four of every 10 women in Jharkhand are undernourished (Singh, sunil 2004).

Table : 07.05

Distribution on the basis of tribal women reported problems during pregnancy

Response	Chiniya	Bhandariya	Total
Yes	538	114	652(51.25%)
No	208	412	620(49.75%)
Total	**746**	**526**	**1272**
If yes, 7.5.1	**Y-538**	**Y-114**	**652**
Night blindness	352	48	400(28.53%)
Haziness	90	4	94(6.10%)
Convulsions	30	-	30(0.21%)
Swelling	244	28	272(19.40%)
Obesity	234	46	280(19.97%)
Anaemia	296	28	324(23.10%)
Others	-	2	2(0.14%)
Total	**1246**	**156**	**1402(100%)**

Note- In the above table tribal women reported more than one problems so the percentage may exceed.

In the table no. 07.05, it was asked to the respondents during pregnancy they got some physical or other kind of problems. Out of the total respondents (652) 28.53% women reported that they had problem of night blindness. 6.70% respondents told they were feeling haziness. 0.21% reported about the problem of convulsions, 19.40% reported about swelling of body. 19.97% told about lots of weight during pregnancy. 23.10% reported Anaemia in their body. 0.14% had suffered from some others problems during pregnancy.

Table : 07.06

Distribution of tribal women agencies vaccination given by agencies

agencies	Chiniya	Bhandariya	Total
Govt.	94	6	100(3.21%)
Health	82	36	118(3.79%)

Private	-	-	-
Polio booth	1634	970	2604(83.83%)
Others	102	182	284(9.14%)
Total	**1912**	**1194**	**3106(100%)**

In the table no. 07.06, when it was asked to the respondents which agency has given vaccination to children, out of total respondents (3106), 83.83% respondents told their children got polio drops from polio booth. 3.21% and 3.79% respondents reported government hospitals and health camps were the major agencies for vaccination respectively. Only 9.14% respondents were dependent on others agencies.

Table : 07.07

Distribution of tribal women treatment given when children are ill

Response	Chiniya	Bhandariya	Total
Jhadfhunk	58	40	98 (7.70%)
Treatment	622	410	1032
Both	66	76	142
Total	**746 (58.65%)**	**526 (41.36%)**	**1272 (100%)**

In the table no. 07.07, with regard to children health it was important to know the treatment facilities respondents used when their children are sick or in case of general disease? 81.13% women said they take their own domestic treatment for sick children. 7.70% respondents dependent on Jhad-phook and Jaado-toona or informal means. 11.16% respondents used both Jhad-Phook and treatment for their children when they are ill.

Table : 07.08

Distribution of frequency of diseases in tribal women's children

Diseases	Chiniya	Bhandariya	Total
Cough /cold	282	294	576
Phenomena	290	208	498

Diarrhoea	250	10	260
others	162	174	336
Total	984	686	1670
M	m-1.3	m-1.3	m-1.3

In the table no. 07.08, with regard to know which diseases more frequently attack on children of respondents, an average of each item of categories taken for analysis. Out of total disease frequency 1.3 averages of diseases make children sick due to cough and cold, Diarrhoea.

More than 20% of the children in Jharkhand suffer from diarrhoea and acute respiratory infections. More than half of the children (56%) suffer from moderate to severe anaemia. Less than 10% of the children aged 12-23 months are fully immunized. About one-third of children do not receive any immunization at all.

Reproductive Health

The proportion of pregnant women receiving antenatal check-ups in Jharkhand is quite low as only 10 women receive at least one antenatal check-up. Only one-third of pregnant women receive IFA tablets. More than three-fourths of deliveries that take place in the state are unsafe. Nearly nine out of ten deliveries take place at home.

Table : 07.09

Distributions of tribal women do deliveries in hospital

No of children	Chiniya	Bhandariya	Total
1	40	4	44 (3.45%)
2	54	-	54 (4.24%)
3	12	-	12 (0.94%)
4	2	-	2 (0.15%)
None	638	522	1160 (91.19%)
Total	746 (58.65%)	526 (41.36%)	1272 (100%)

In the above table no. 07.09, it was asked to respondents that how many children born in the hospitals? Out of the total respondents, 91.19% respondents reported that no any childrens born in hospital. 3.45% respondents said their only one child was born in hospital. 4.24% said two children were born in hospital. Negligible number of respondents said 3-4 children were delivered in hospital with 0.94% and 0.15% respectively.

Family planning

In connection with the institution of marriage it is necessary to make an enquiry into the matter of family planning among the tribal women. The number of the planned families is an index of advancement on the part of the citizens and also an index of the amount of success on the part of the government. The problem of population has assumed the top most priority and many hectic efforts are being made by the government to control the population explosion. On the other side the question of awakening is also important because unless the people come to know the importance of the population problem, the plans of the government will not be fully successful. Only a quarter of the currently married women in Jharkhand use modern method of contraception. About 38% of the currently married are using modern method of contraception compared with 22% rural women. Female sterilization dominates the method mix (88%). Less than 1% of the couples use male sterilization.

Table : 07.10

Distributions of respondent awareness of family planning methods

Response	Chiniya	Bhandariya	total
Yes	640	226	866 (68.08%)
No	106	300	406 (31.91%)
Total	746 (58.65%)	526 (41.36%)	1272 (100%)
If yes, 7.10-1	**Y-640**	**Y-226**	**Total Y -866**
T.V.	-	26	26(3.0)
Radio	20	36	56(6.46)
Anganwadi	262	100	362(41.80)
Asha	190	-	190(12.19)
Others	138	94	232(26.78)
Total	**652**	**256**	**866(100)**

There are 866 respondents (68.8%) who have awareness of family planning methods were under study. 31.91% respondents were not aware of methods of family planning. Among 866 respondents were asked from where they got information about methods of family planning. Out of total respondents, 3.0% took information from television, 6.46% got information from Radio announcement, 41.80% respondents informed by aganwadi workers, 2.19% got information through ASHA, 26.78% got awareness from other sources of information.

Table : 07.11

Distributions of tribal women family practicing planning

Methods	Chiniya			Bhandariya			Total
	Used	Heard	Don't know	Used	Heard	Don't know	
Injection / tablets	330	234	28	78	188	84	942
Condom/nirodh	146	390	72	16	238	98	960
IUD / loop	2	348	162	-	244	96	852
Tubectomy	178	464	4	36	244	76	1002
Vasectomy	2	582	8	2	266	72	932
Safe period / others	2	266	10	106	62	48	494
Total	660	2284	284	238	1242	474	5182
M	0.88	3.06	0.38	0.45	2.36	0.90	4.07

In the table no. 07.11, when it was asked to respondents whether they know about various methods of family planning an average or mean was taken of each group to know frequency of methods of family planning. Methods of family planning 0.88 average respondents used these methods, 30.6 average respondents only heard about two to three methods of family planning, 0.38 average female don't know about these methods in Chiniya block. With regard to Bhandariya block, 0.45 average respondents used these methods, 2.36 average respondents heard about it. Only 0.90 average people don't know about methods of family planning.

Table : 07.12

Reasons of tribal women not practicing family planning

Reasons	Chiniya	bhandariya	Total
Method is not	4	14	18 (4.81%)
Unsafe	2	26	28 (7.48%)
Born children	28	54	82 (21.92%)
Health problem	12	20	32(8.55%)
Others	40	174	214
Total	**86** **(22.99%)**	**288** **(77.00%)**	**374 (100%)**

As above table 07.12 shows, the total number of the respondents who have not undergone family planning is 374. Out of them 4.81%respondents said these methods are not good. 7.48% told that family planning methods are unsafe for health. 21.92% respondents revealed that they want more children. 8.55% respondents told they have some health related problem to accept it. 57.21% respondents said there are some other reasons for not practicing these family planning methods.

Table : 07.13

Distributions of Tribal Women facilities provided by govt.

Block	* 1	* 2	* 3	1	2	3	Total
	Yes			No			
Chiniya	432			314			746 (58.65%)
Bhandari ya	152			374			526 (41.36%)
total	584 (45.91%)			688 (54.08%)			1272 (100%)

* Explanation

* Vaccine

* Nutritional food

* Iron folic

159

In the table no. 07.13, with regard to the services, benefits provided by government to the pregnant women. Out of the 584 (45.91%) respondents in both block Chiniya and Bhandariya told they were provided Vaccines, Nutritional food and Iron folic by the government.

Political Participation and Decision Making

The tribes have their own village or jati (caste) panchayat which was more effective in the past. In the olden days the panchayat had been called traditional panchayat. The main functions of traditional or jati (caste) panchayat are: (a) to see that no one violates the customary laws, (b) to collect the rent from the raiyats, (c) to get the deities appeased in time so that no calamity befalls the village and (d) to look after the welfare and development of the tribes' men. The official of the panchayat is a head man known as Pradhan (Sahay K. K., 2005:P 142).

Table : 07.14

Do you have caste panchayat in your caste

Response	Chiniya	Bhandariya	Total
Yes	540	398	938 (73.75%)
No	206	128	334 (26.26%)
Total	**746 (58.65%)**	**526 (41.36%)**	**1272 (100%)**

The above table no. 07.14 shows the extent of political participation of 1272 respondents under study. Out of the total respondents, 73.75% replied that they had caste panchayat in their village. 26.26% respondents told they did not have any caste panchayat in their village.

Another important aspect of the political conditions of any particular community is the selection of leader for voting purpose. Different people have different choices if they are highly educated and independent in their decision and

160

judgement. Because in the present study it is found majority of the respondents are illiterate and do not take much interest in politics.

Table : 07.15

Distribution of the Tribal Women showing selection of leader

Response	Chiniya	Bhandariya	Total
Yes	262	0	262 (20.6%)
No	484	526	972 (76.42%)
Total	**746 (58.65%)**	**526 (41.36%)**	**1272 (100%)**

In the above mentioned table 07.15, when it was asked to the respondents how they select their leader, 76.42% respondents replied they select their leader by election, only 20.6% respondents told selection of leader is made through hereditary.

Table : 07.16

Distribution of the Tribal Women Showing Membership of Family Member in Caste Panchayat

Response	Chiniya	Bhandariya	Total
Yes	192	28	220 (17.3%)
No	554	498	1052 (82.71%)
Total	**746 (58.65%)**	**526 (41.36%)**	**1272 (100%)**

This table no.07.16 depicts the number of respondents' family members involved in political affairs. 82.71% respondents negatively replied that they have no any member from their family in the caste panchayat. Only few 17.3% respondents said they have family members in caste panchayat.

161

Table : 07.17

Distribution of the Tribal Women Permission of Membership of Female in Caste Panchayat

Response	Chiniya	Bhandariya	Total
Yes	48	302	350 (27.52%)
No	698	224	922 (72.49%)
Total	746 (58.65%)	526 (41.36%)	1272 (100%)

The analysis of the above table no. 07.17 throws light on the facts that 72.49% respondents are not allowed to have membership in the caste panchayat. 27.52% respondents said they are permitted to have membership in the caste panchayat.

It is common among the tribal societies that elders share their powers with the officials of the panchayat in its deliberation. Women and children are not eligible to take part in the caste panchayat.

Majority of the women among the selected community of tribes follow the advice of some particular persons and cast their votes, with least regard for the principles, historical background and achievement of either the party or the candidate. Although majority of the respondents exercise their franchise though they have neither definite political conviction nor political ambitions. They do not know exactly whom they should vote for and why? They usually exercise their franchise under external pressure, relation with the candidate contesting the election or by caste affinity and so on.

Table : 07.18

Distribution of the Tribal Women showing participation in election of leader

Response	Chiniya	Bhandariya	Total
Yes	230	218	448 (35.23%)
No	516	308	824 (64.78%)
Total	746 (58.65%)	526 (41.36%)	1272 (100%)

On the basis of the table no. 07.18 participation of respondents in candidate contesting election, 35.23% respondents replied positively and 64.78% respondents replied negatively that they do not participate in the election of leader.

Keeping the above mechanism in view, the researcher included a few questions in the schedule to gather information whether the respondents had approached the panchayat's officers or any other individual to represent their problem and to get them solved.

Table : 07.19

Distribution on the basis of Panchayat intervention

Matters	Chiniya	Bhandariya	Total
spousal	2	30	32 (2.5%)
Marriage	242	118	360 (28.13%)
Family dispute	504	384	888 (69.38%)
Total	748 (58.44%)	532 (41.57%)	1280 (100%)

On the basis of above table (07.19), 69.38% respondents said that political parties intervene in the family disputes. 28.13% respondents said that caste panchayat advised in arrangement of marriage in their family. Only 2.5% respondents said that they go for panchayat when they have fight with husband.

Table : 07.20

Distribution of the Tribal Women taking opinion in political matters

Matters	Chiniya	Bhandariya	Total
Caste leader	22	54	76 (5.93%)
Religious leader	12	22	34 (2.66%)
Respected person	620	362	982 (76.6%)
Family members	102	88	190 (14.83%)
Total	756 (58.98%)	526 (41.03%)	1282 (100%)

In the above table 07.20 it shows that respondents have poor knowledge about political field or politics. However their participation in politics is of different forms. When it was asked to respondents from whom they take advice to select the political leader apart from caste panchayat to cast their votes. 76.6% respondents said they take advice from the respected person or key person of their village. 14.83% respondents take advice from their family members. 5.93% respondents take opinion from caste leader and 2.66% take advice from religious leader or the village priest.

Table : 07.21

Distribution of the Tribal Women casting vote

Response	Chiniya	Bhandariya	Total
Yes	692	346	1038 (81.6%)
No	54	180	234 (18.4%)
Total	**746 (58.65%)**	**526 (41.36%)**	**1272 (100%)**

In table no. 07.21 the data reveals that 81.6% respondents cast their votes. 18.4% respondents do not cast their vote as they are not interested in politics.

Table : 07.22

Distribution of the basis of Tribal Women having any card

Types of card	Chiniya	Bhandariya	Total
Ration card	356	136	492 (29.47%)
Voter card	566	416	982 (58.81%)
Blow poverty line	160	30	190 (11.38%)
Others	2	4	6 (0.36%)
Total	**1084 (64.92%)**	**586 (35.09%)**	**1670 (100%)**
M	**m-1.4**	**m-1.1**	**m-1.3**

The above table no. 07.22 indicates that number of respondents are beneficiaries of privilege cards. Under this study respondents revealed that they have more than two or three cards. The mean or an average have been taken from total population, 58.81% respondents have their voter ID cards. 29.47% respondents have ration cards, 11.38% respondents have below poverty line (BPL) cards. Only 0.36% respondents have some other cards.

Table : 07.23

Distribution of the Tribal Women awareness of Government Schemes

Response	Chiniya	Bhandariya	Total
Yes	666	266	932 (73.28%)
No	80	260	340 (26.73%)
Total	746 (58.65%)	526 (41.36%)	1272 (100%)

The above table no. 07.23, shows that out of the total selected respondents, 73.28% are aware about the government schemes which are running for betterment or for benefit of tribals 26.73% respondents are not aware about the government programmes and policies for the tribals' development.

Table : 07.24

Distribution of the Tribal Women taken benefits

Response	Chiniya	Bhandariya	Total
Yes	580	162	742 (58.34%)
No	166	364	530 (41.67%)
Total	746 (58.65%)	526 (41.36%)	1272 (100%)

The table no. 07.24 indicates that the number of the respondents benefitted and not-benefitted by the government policies and programmes. While 58.34% respondents are benefitted from the government programmes, 41.67% respondents are not taken benefits from the government programmes. Developmental programmes of central as well as state government are also greatly responsible for the changing conditions of the tribes under study.

Distribution of the Tribal Women taken benefits from given programmes

	Chiniya	Bhandariya	Total
Kanyadan yajana	6	2	8 (0.5%)
Inter caste	2	-	2 (0.1%)
Scholarship	184	52	236
Cycles	154	62	216 (14.4%)
Financial	4	4	8 (0.5%)
Indira awas	88	28	116 (7.74%)
Animals	4	-	4 (0.2%)
Grains	472	424	896
Agricultural	10	2	12 (0.8%)
others	2	-	2 (0.1%)
Total	**926**	**574**	**1500**
M	**m-1.2**	**m-1.0**	**m-1.1**

The above table no. 07.25 shows that the importance of various beneficiary cards carry by the respondents, 59.74% respondents have taken grains and cereals from their block office. 15.74% respondents had taken scholarship for education of their children, 14.4% had taken bicycle for their children, 7.74% had taken benefits from Indira Awas Yojana (IAY) and negligible number of respondents were benefited from kanyadan Yojana. agricultural, animals related benefits.

Decision-making is important in management because it is the way we make things happen instead of just letting them happen. Decision making forms the central activity pattern or core of the management process, as resources (means) are used to attain goals lends in living day to day, year and for a life time. In male dominated societies the process of decision making is normally dominated by the male members. There is a belief prevailing in male dominated societies that women are inferior creatures, incapable of taking decisions as properly as the male members. Tribal women still play subordinate role (Sinha, Rekha & Vdai: 2007 P. 135).

Table : 07.26

Distribution of the Tribal Women showing decision making in family

Matters	Chiniya				Bhandariya				Total
	Self	Husband	Elder	Others	Self	Husband	Old	Others	
children marriage Related	30	392	316		12	134	88	-	972
Education related	250	502	10	2	32	216	-	-	1012
Purchasing grocery	414	316	12	-	164	118	-	-	1024
Property related	32	644	28	-	8	232	12	-	956
Agriculture related	102	592	28	-	32	220	2	-	976
Debt related	154	556	10	-	36	214	-	-	970
Saving related	414	298	20	-	86	162	-	-	980
Personal matters	58	302	172	-	24	118	78	2	754
Others	4	36	-	-	2	16	4	-	62
Total	**1458**	**3638**	**596**	**2**	**396**	**1430**	**184**	**2**	**7706**
	m-1.9	**m-4.8**	**0.7**	**0.0**	**0.7**	**2.7**	**0.3**	**0.0**	**6.0**

Decision making of respondents in matters of family is an important indicator of status of women, as decision making process defines their strong role or exploitation and regard of her decision in her family. In above table no. 07.25 it shows that decisions by self, husband, old and others are made in 4 groups and matters were given. Another side, an average of each items and groups represented in table 1.9 averages, respondents told decision by them given in one to two matters husband takes four to five decision with 4.8 average, elders or aged people with 0.7 average take decision in family in the selected Chiniya and Bhandariya blocks. 0.7 average. An average 2.7 husbands take decision in every matter. The categories of matters are, children marriage-related aspect, education-related, purchasing grocery, property-related, agriculture-related, debt-related, saving-related, personal matter etc.

REFERENCES

➢ Chaudhary, Anita   (2012): 'Empowerment of Rural Women: Issues and Oppertunities', Akhand Publishing House, New Delhi, P. 104,117.

➢ Sinha, Rekha & Udai: (2007) :'Women Empowerment and Family Management in Tribal Region', Concept Publishing company, New Delhi. P. 135

➢ Sahay, K. K.,   (2005) :'Development of goand tribes in modern perspective', Classical Publishing Company. New Delhi, p.142.

CHAPTER – VIII
FINDINGS AND RECOMMENDATIONS

I.   Developing countries of Third World are housing the largest tribal population of the world. India, among the South-Asian countries, is having largest number of tribal's numbering over 80 million. In other words, India has highest concentration of tribal population next to Africa and before Myanmar. Few tribal groups in Africa, India and Myanmar have embraced Christianity, Islam, Buddhism, etc. These tribal groups are in the process of modernization. Due to embracing different religions, they are losing their tribal identity. As far as distribution of Scheduled Tribe population is concerned, the entire Scheduled Tribe population of India is divided into different zones such as North-eastern, Northeast, central, Western, South and Islands, The population of Scheduled Tribes are not in habiting in Punjab, Haryana, Delhi, Chandigarh and Pondicherry due to geographical and cultural reasons. In India, 432 tribal communities are living in above-mentioned different parts of the country. Tribal populations in India are largely concentrated in Madhya Pradesh, Chhattisgarh, Jharkhand, Gujarat, Rajasthan, Maharashtra, Andhra-Pradesh, etc. Gond, Bhil, Santhal, Oraon are some of the largest tribal groups of India. The tribal population of India inhabit in forest and remote areas and have been largely depending on forest. They follow primitive method of agriculture. Besides forest and agriculture, tribals are involved in labour, agriculture and casual labour along with cattle rearing, mining and quarrying, etc., to maintain their livelihood.

Jharkhand has a population of 26.93 million, consisting of 13.88 million males and 13.08 million females. The sex ratio is 941 females to 1000 males. The population consists of 28% tribal's, 12% scheduled caste and 60% other. There are 274 persons for each square kilometer of land. However, the population density varies considerably from as low as 148 per square kilometer in Gumla district to as high as 1167 per square kilometer in Dhanbad district. Around 10% of the population is Bengali speaking and 70% speak various dialect of Hindi. The tribes of Jharkhand consist of 32 tribes inhabiting in Jharkhand state of India. The tribes in Jharkhand were originally classified on the basis of their cultural types by the world renowned Indian anthropologist late professor L. P. Vidhyarthi Classified tribes are as follows:

1. Hunter gatherer type – Birhor Korwa, Hill Korwa,

2. Shifting agriculture – Sauria Paharia

3. Simple artisans - mahli,lohra,karmali,chik baraik

4. Setteled agriculturists –santhal,munda,oraon,ho,bhumij,etc.

Jharkhand is famous for its rich mineral resources like Uranium, Mica, Bauxite, Granite Gold, Silver, Coal (32% of India), Iron, Copper (25% of India) etc. Forests and woodlands occupy more than 29% of the state which is amongst the highest in India.

In this chapter many important tribes in India are dealt with for the purpose of understanding the distinguishing features of the tribals and also to trace out the common traits among them since all the tribals are Indians geographically and from the national point of view. They are subject to the common dynamic forces acting upon their economic and political conditions. In this connection an extensive study of literature has been instituted and the different opinions and descriptions of the eminent authors were taken into consideration so as to form a clear and comprehensive estimate of the tribal life in India.

Women play a significant role in tribal economy. Women work more in tribal society compared to their counterpart men. Tribal women have been engaging in collection of minor forest produce, medicinal herbs, tuber, fodder, grass, charcoal, fuel wood, etc. After selling these items, they use to purchase other basis requirements like matchbox, kerosene, salt, sugar, cloths, etc. Women in tribal society are considered as equal economic partners and decisions-makers. Women in fact work hard performing dual role in the domestic and productive role besides bearing and rearing of children. In India there are 75 tribal groups identified as Primitive Tribal Group. The Primitive Tribal Groups have got low level of literacy, declining or stagnant nature of population with primitive method of agriculture, which put them in economic backwardness. All these tribal groups are small in number and are living in remote areas and interior places with poor administrative and infrastructure support.

In the first part of the chapter the field study is introduced with reference to its historical past, geographical conditions, demographic aspect of the tribes in India. After that characteristics definitions of tribes, meaning of different tribes are covered in this chapter. In the chapter conditions and vulnerable aspects of tribal women are also discussed. Tribal women face the various kinds of problems in their life span.

II. In the second chapter of the project, with respect to the tribals the overview of part literature nationally and internationally taken into consideration in detail so that the operational definitions which were given in this chapter could be understood clearly. In this connection an extensive study of literature has been instituted and different opinions and descriptions of the eminent authors were taken into consideration so as to form a clear and comprehensive estimate of the tribal life in India.

III. In the third chapter of research study, study area, importance of study, need of the study, research design have been taken into consideration. The tribal women of Garhwa district are also like other groups of society and are in low status than men and what reason is an interesting for the study and investigation. Therefore, the researcher has selected the subject of tribal women of Garhwa district to find out the causes and problems of tribal women which are responsible for low socio-economic status among tribal women.

Therefore, a thorough study of the actual conditions of the tribal women being found necessary to find out the truths and represent them before the government and the tribal people.

The subject of the study states as follows "A study of socio-economic status of tribes of Jharkhand state with special reference to women".

It is a descriptive-cum-explorative study delimited by its research design. However, the findings of the study summarized in next chapter as follows:-

Objectives

1. To know the socio-economic profile of the tribal women.
2. To analyse the educational status of tribal girls.
3. To study the nature of economic empowerment and migration and related exploitation of tribal women.
4. To know the extent of crime against tribal women and girls.
5. To evaluate the participation of tribal women in the development programme executed by government.

Methodology

This study has been carried out in Chiniya and Bhandariya blocks of (Garhwa district of Jharkhand state). The method of study was by survey and observation of the selected area from the sociological point of view. Investigation and enquiry were based on interview Schedule. Prepared by the investigator after a pilot survey the questions were simple, straight and direct and graded in different parts, so as to over all the important aspects of the past and present status of tribal women.

Simultaneously with approaches to the respondents the researcher visited some of the concerned offices co-operative and panchayat committee secretaries to collect information and also to verify some of the particular information provided by the respondents. Primary data was collected by a team of female investigators deputed in each block covered by the study. The secondary data was collected by the principal investigator and the project fellowed. The data collected was edited, processed and analysed with the help of computers. Thus on the basis of primary and secondary data collected, statistical statement was prepared and conclusions were drawn.

The entire information and the critical observation there upon were put in black and white in the form of a project report which is divided into eight chapters, entitled as follows.

1. Status of tribals in India.
2. Overview of literature.
3. Research methodology.
4. Profile of study area and social status of the tribal women.

5. Economic status of the tribal women.
6. Work participation gender discrimination and exploitation.
7. Health status and political participation.
8. Conclusion and suggestion.

Annexure are also enclosed at the end of the project report, interview schedule, maps etc.

The study comprises sample of the 1272 tribal women belonged to above mentioned villages falling under two different blocks, Chiniya and Bhandaria. Out of the total population of both blocks, 746 tribal women of Chiniya block and 526 tribal women of Bhandaria block were selected on the basis of stratified sampling method. The interviews of all the 1272 tribal women were conducted and organized through pre-tested interview Schedule.

IV. Social status and Profile of Tribal Women

In respect of the social conditions of the household and respondents, the profile of study area and respondents were taken into consideration.

In this chapter the social conditions of the tribal women are delineated on the basis of the selected household of both Chiniya and Bhandariya blocks.

Family aspect is the next topic in the chapter. Under this aspect the size of the family based on the range of the members in each, the distribution of the tribal women according to the size of the family distributed according to the type of the families. Namely Nuclear and Joint families are also provided each aspect in its tabular form with critical analysis. While majority of the respondents were found living in nuclear families (54.24%), less than half of the respondents lived in joint or extended families.

Age at the marriage of each respondent is also known through the interview schedule. It is observed that there are six (group) categories of respondents in this regard. Majority of tribal women (37.57%) are between the age of twenty six to thirty five of age group. 31.28% respondents were in the age of thirty six to forty five of age group.

The sub tribe of the tribal women is: 1. Kharwar, 2. Parhiya, 3. Korwa, 4. other tribes. Majority of tribal women 74.69% respondents were belonging to Kharwar sub tribe.

Family aspect is the next topic for explanation in this study. In family size total population of selected blocks (Chiniya and Bhandaria) taken in to consideration with the population of total male member including boys and girls were also included in this table. Total population of selected families was 60.91% in Chiniya block and 39.10% in Bhandaria block.

More than 55.35% of tribal women were illiterate. About 31.29% and 6.29% respondents respectively were literate and educated up to primary level. Only 4.41% respondents were found secondary passed and 2.68% respondents were high school passed.

Literacy rate of this Garhwa district is 39.39% in which male literacy rate is 54.69% as against the female literacy rate 22.9%. This district has poor literacy rate as against the average literacy rate (54.13) of Jharkhand state.

Marriage is another important aspect to know the social life of respondents. Marital status was categorized in four groups, married, widow, abandoned and divorcee. Majority of women 85.85% respondents were married. 13.68% respondents were widow. Only 13.68% women were abaunded. No woman was found unmarried as marriage at early age is solemnised in the tribal culture. The system of marriage in tribal culture is most important. It is observed during interviews of respondents. That bride-price system has lost its ground and in its place dowry is gaining ground. Money, gold, silver and some time other kinds are also offered as dowry.

V.   Economic status

Economic background of tribal women disclosed that a large majority of them depended on agriculture and labour for their livelihood. They have undergone considerable changes on account of their gradual merging in the general society. In many cases in the place of caste occupation, they have agriculture and agriculture labour.

Under the economic status the following are the important aspects taken into consideration.

1. Occupation
2. Income
3. Land holding
4. Dwelling house
5. Patterns of housing
6. Expenditure
7. Animal domestication
8. Loans
9. Utility of goods etc.

Under the first aspect of economic status in the traditional occupations 27.21 and 26.45% tribal women depend on agriculture, agriculture labour respectively. About 25.74% and 9.91% tribal women do animal husbandry and others work as bonded labour respectively. Tribal women also depend on handicraft and traditional work.

The income of the respondents in the next consideration under economic status, categories of income are made ranging from less than Rs. 5000. And Rs. 6000-15000, 16000-25000, 26000-35000 and above, it is observed that highest number of respondents 552 (43.39%) are in the group of Rs. 16000-25000. Only 18 (1.41%) respondents are in the group of Rs. 26000-35000.

In the next table, land holdings are distributed on the basis of acres, less than one acre, two to three acres, four to five acres, six to seven acres, eight to nine acres and above ten acres. The highest number 550 (43.24%) respondents were found under the two to three acres. Another highest number 394 (30.98%) respondents were under the less than one acres land holding.

In the next aspect of economic status, ownership of house have been considered. Highest number of respondents 1256 (98.75%) live in their own house not as a tenant. In addition to ownership of house, number of rooms in house is also very important to know the individual space in house for respondents. Highest number (46.70%, 594) respondents have one to two rooms in their home. Second highest number (38.06%, 484) respondents have three rooms to four rooms in their home.

Housing condition includes separate place for kitchen, all civil amenities such as water, electricity, latrines, bathrooms and proper ventilation. An attempt was made by the study team to analyze the availability of those amenities in the houses of tribal women living in villages. Highest number of respondents 1014 (79.72%) have no separate place for kitchen in their house which resulted in carbonated smoke, causing various diseases including Asthma and Cancer.

Similarly, household utensils, type of metals by which utensils are made, fuel consumption in the house indicates the economic status of tribal women.

Another important aspect is related to farm expenditure, sources of irrigation, additional work done by the respondents to generate more money by collecting the forest residue.

In the description of the animals and bird domesticated by the respondents have taken into account. Rearing of sheep and goats, cattle are also secondary sources of income. It is observed that majority of respondents 888 (27.93%) reared the ox for farming, 872 (27.43%) domesticate goat for milk and for selling. In the next table expenditure on various items in the family is indicated. While highest number 8750 (41.10%) of respondents spend money on food, 5545 (26.05%) spend money on cloths and lowest number 510 (2.39%) of respondents spend money on cosmetics.

In the next table the loan position is described and also the total amount of loan borrowed is shown through different categories for farming, marriage, education, medicine, religion, crops for purchasing animals.

While the highest loan amount 10433 (20.39%) is borrowed by the respondents, for farming the lowest amount 2607 (5.09%) after crops were not produced in the farms.

The primary data collected from the respondents disclosed that garment which is wear by the respondents is saree with 98.3% as well as they wear salwar-suits and gown (maxi) it was also observed due to the availability of various kinds of clothes, majority of respondents 708 (41.26%) wear cotton clothes, followed by polyester, tricot and others texture of clothes.

It is also important to indicate that respondents of selected villages purchase clothes yearly ranging from one to three or more. Majority of respondents 684 (53.53%) purchase only one clothes yearly which shows their low economic condition and purchasing capacity.

In the last place of the chapter, items of luxury owned by the respondents are taken into consideration. The respondents of the selected villages in fact, have no leisure as they spend all their time in the activities which are connected with their occupations and livelihood amenities. Majority of respondents have only 35.46% cots. 22.44% (734) respondents have choki and 15.78% (516) have chairs in their home. It is also important to indicate that due to advance methods of communication and easy accessibility of mobile phones, 314 (9.6%) respondents have mobile phone for communication to their relatives. Basic amenities like watch, cooker, water pump and hand pump in house, sewing machine are found in most of the house.

The primary data collected from the respondents disclosed the tribal women large their pattern of clothing, pattern of living and items of luxuries possessed by the respondents.

VI. Work Exploitation and Discrimination

It is well accepted that women in rural areas work more than their counterpart men. They get up early in the morning and work throughout the day and they are the last in the family to go to bed which lasts hardly four to five hours in the whole duration of the day and night. In India, unemployment among women is higher than men. Since Independence, Government of India has created enough employment opportunities for women under different five year plan (Sikligar. 31). In this study, field investigator also examined tribal women's employment status, income range and level of exploitation both financial and sexual. In the table of working status of tribal women, it was observed that majority of tribal women working under in MGNREGA (Mahatma Gandhi National Rural Employment Guarantee Act.). 67.46%. Scheme provides them employment under the MGNREGA. Women working do not get timely payment as 55.35% respondent told about it. It is important to mention here that under MGNREGA, tribal women working as a daily wages labour do not get 624 (49.06%) full payment equal to men worker which shows their gender discrimination. In the next table an attempt was made to collect the information about the work load of tribal women, their participation in household work. It was observed that women do rearing of children. cooking food, washing, clothes, cutting woods, cleaning of house, cattle's caring, caring of aged family member, marketing too. Due to household chores they do not get time for caring themselves. Majority of women do another work when there is no season of cultivation in farms. Respondents also disclosed this fact that when they do not have any secondary source of income they migrate to another place or region or state in search of employment. Majority of number 552 (43.33%) respondents migrate when there is no season of cultivation. Tribal women also 26 (2.05%) work as house maid in others houses. Some times they are seasonally migrated and sometime permanently when they get enough money.

Most of the respondents do another traditional work as basket making, hand fans making, beedi making with (13.19%). It is important to know (176 13.82%) respondents were dependent on others income.

An attempt was made to collect information about the sexual exploitation and gender discrimination of respondents in family or outside. The principal causes of financial and sexual exploitation of the tribal women were poverty, lack of employment opportunities, unorganized nature of labour force, misunderstanding of family members, husbands, neighbors' and relatives.

In the next table respondents disclosed that in their family both boys and girls share responsibilities of family members. Highest number of boys and girls 3012 (34.54%) help parents in agriculture work. 3830 (22.7%) boys and girls help in household work too.

Some of respondents said that their children work as a servant 234 (2.68%) in others home who economically well sound.

In the next table respondent disclosed that majority of children go to school but some of them do not go to school as respondents reported this situation is due to lack of awareness among tribal communities about the scheme of state and central governments for providing free education to the tribal boys and girls. Another factor is that majority of parents live in rural and remote areas where they do not get much priority of education for their girl child. Moreover, they involve girl child in all types of household activities including rearing of younger brother and sister. While parents go to fields or work apart from such problems, many parents migrate seasonwise which inculcate in minds of their parents not to show much interest for education of their children, particularly girl child (Silkligar, 2006.33).

Majority of children 278 (30.95%) do not know the reason why they do not study. 24.49% children have responsibility of younger brothers and sisters, 13.80% share house hold work.

With regard to the prior mentioned secondary data about violence against women, in the chapter six, respondents reported that they are victim of domestic violence but respondents hesitated to disclose their married life. Only 350 (27.52%) respondent have revealed quarrel with their husband, the reasons of domestic violence of respondents were 174 (49.72%) told that their husband are alcohal addict and other type of narcotics (morphine) 22.86% told that husband has suspicious nature and always suspect about her behavior. Tribal women also disclosed the fact that family member and husband feel that she is not efficient to do household work which is another reason of fighting. Some respondents said they think their husband is cheating with them, he has illegal relation with other women. So these are the important factors of domestic violence with the spouses of tribal women.

Besides the exploitation by husband, respondents were exploited by others with 468 (36.8%) respondents have been victim of sexual harassment by others or outsider.

The respondents were hesitating to report the facts about sexual exploitation. As a result, only 14.16% of women disclosed that they had been victims of sexual harassment in the form of verbal comment by family member (38.89%), relatives

(20.56%), neighbors (29.45%), by landlord (11.12%). The comments given by them e.g. she does not cook food (13.89%), she cannot give birth a baby boy (18.34%), want to make physical relation with her (4.45%), she cannot make food properly (11.12%), she is witch (21.12%). With regard to sexual exploitation respondents hesitatingly reported 35.38% have been tried by any male to make physical relations.

In the next table related to women exploitation, another form of harassment is more prevalent in the tribal community, e.g. witch crafting or hunting. Under the selected villages of research study, respondents were asked that any woman had been paraded nude in their village, only 3.94% hesitatingly answered about this incident and with regard to practice of witch hunting under the study, only 13.53% respondents revealed that witch practicing was happened.

The major reasons came into focus of witch hunting were practice of black magic (28.49%), that woman makes villagers sick (20.94%), frightened people in the village 18.03%. Respondents also said that these women tortured other family members too.

In the next table of this chapter about exploitation of tribal women, many cases came into focus about human trafficking in which poor, vulnerable, needy, innocent women and girls have been sold or purchased in some region of the state. To know about the human trafficking, tribal women of selected research area did not answered properly. Only 13.21% women told that they heard about this incident. Rape is an act of terror that violates a woman's body, space and self-respect through which a woman is systematically made to feel inferior, weak and afraid. Negligible number of respondents reported about the incident of rape happened in their community with 8.97%. Here, it is important to mention about incidents of elope, 31.91% respondents told that tribal girls and women were eloped by villagers.

Cultural and social factors are interlinked with the development and propagation of violent behavior. With different processes of socialization that men and women undergo, men take up stereotyped gender roles of domination and control, whereas women take up that of submission, dependence and respect for authority. A female child grows up with a constant sense of being weak and in need of protection, whether physical, social or economic. This helplessness has led to her exploitation at almost every stage of life (Chaudhary Anita: 2012, 57).

VII. Health and Political Participation

Health is the important indicator of women status in the society. Under this study with regard to health it has been found tribal women are still not very much aware about the health facilities provided by the government. It is seen that majority of women 61.28% respondent still go to Jhola Chhap Doctor (Ojhas) for treatment in illness.

Under the study 39.30% tribal women have reported reproductive health related problems as white discharge (33.6%), stomach ache (32.4%), burning feet etc. it was observed that about maternal mortality rate in early marriage, frequency and repeated childbearing and discrimination faced throughout the life cycle results in adverse health outcomes like. RTI/ STIS, uterine, prolapsed etc. (Anita, 2012, P. 117). It was also observed that majority of tribal women got pregnant two to four times (38.83%), and five to six times (20.19%).

Due to repeated child bearing and marriage at early age. Tribal women reported that they are anemic, night blindness (28.53%), swelling of body and obesity problem.

It is important to mention here, tribal women think that taking vaccine of polio is enough. Tribal women had taken polio vaccination (83.83%) by polio booth due to unfeasibility of hospitals and health centres. They are dependent on camps and booths for vaccination. When children of tribal women become ill or sick, they called Ojhas or do Jadoo-Tona for treatment. But now they are adopting allopathic medicine (81.13%). Children of tribal women suffer from diseases like pneumonia, diarrhea and cough and cold due to unhealthy living conditions and unhygienic food practices.

It is observed that only 3.45% respondents delivered children in hospital. About 31.91% of the respondents do not know family planning methods. Majority of women (68.08%) are well known about family planning. They got information about family planning (41.80%) from anganwadi 12.19% from ASHA 26.78% and rest from other sources. Data shows that tribal women have well knowledge about method of family planning such as condoms, IUD, tubectomy, safe period, oral pills etc. Majority of the tribal women reported that family planning method is not good (4.81%), (7.48%)reported unsafe for them, 8.55% said it causes more health problems.

With a view to provide better facilities for respondents the government provides benefits like free vaccines, nutritional foods, Iron folic acids for pregnant women and lactating mothers and also for children.

Political participation of tribal women has been assessed on the basis of tables understudy. Tribal women are interested in voting but most of them have no political rights and duties. It is observed that most of decisions have been taken by their caste panchayats with regard to spousal fightings, marriage related matters, family disputes in the community. Women and children are not allowed to participate in the caste panchayat.

Besides, it is observed that out of total respondents, 14.83% take advice from family member, 76.6% take advice from key person of the village, and 5.93% take advice from caste leader to select political leader of any political party. It is also observed that 81.6% respondents exercise their franchise. Respondents have no powerful and efficient leader of their own community. There is no highly educated and well informed personality of their community to lead them and guide them. Therefore, their political awakening is restricted only to selection of their political leader of concerned party.

About 73.28% respondents are aware about government programmer and schemes. 58.34% respondents take benefits from various schemes such as, Kaanyadan Yojna, Scholarship (15.74%), to provide grains (59.74%), bicycle by government (14.4%), Indira Awas Yojna, agricultural assistance (0.8%) and so on.

Throughout the study, it is observed that the respondents have not been benefited by various facilities like loan facilities, educational facilities, and distribution of excess lands to the landless, employment schemes for the rural unemployment etc. The government has not given special attention to the most backward households of selected village who were the tribals of the jungles and the hills some centuries ago. They are treated along with other backward classes and scheduled castes as though the tribal women are no par with those communities.

With regard to decision making in family matters, tribal women reported that they are not entirely free to take decision regarding every aspect of life, despite the fact that they enjoy more freedom than non-tribal women. Those women, who are sole earner in their family, have more rights to take decisions. In patriarchal tribal societies, women do not enjoy rights to decisions are making. As in the table shown in children's marriage related matters decisions taken by husband and elders. The decision inmatters related to education of children, property related, agriculture-related, debt-related are taken by husband, elders only; matters on purchasing grocery items for mostly done by husbands and wives both.

Recommendation and Suggestions

Women all over the world are subjected to the male domination. In few cases they are given freedom to take decisions on matters related to their personal lives. From time to time society relaxes its grip over the women and that is generally followed by the socio-economic changes. In tribal societies as said earlier the women enjoy a position of equality with men because of their economic potentiality as working partners of their husband. As such, it is expected that they should enjoy more freedom to take decisions on matters relating to their private lives (Sinha, Rekha & Udai: 2007 P. 135).

Some of the important problems of tribal women under study are taken into consideration and the remedial measures are also suggested at some length. Their important problems and suggestions are given below -

1. The tribes of Garhwa district are cultivators or agriculturist as agriculture is the main occupation of the tribes. Although, the tribes of Garhwa district persisting in the traditional style of agriculture and the farming depends upon monsoon. At the hard time respondents have to take loan from Mahajan or other resources and they are indebted.

183

2. Another problem of tribes is indebtedness. They are in poor economic condition. The main reasons of indebtness show that majority of the tribal take loan to meet their agriculture input needs, social and religious ceremonies etc.

3. Illiteracy is rampant among tribal women. Instances of adultery and rape, maltreatment, physical beating and other acts of cruelty are frequently reported. Social insecurity of women is widely reported.

4. There is lack of awareness towards the education due to poverty, so the percentage of literacy in selected blocks of Chiniya & Bhandariya is very low. Thus, some other basic problems of tribe's education are infrastructure of school, medium of instruction, less motivation for education to the children.

5. Majority of the tribal women and girls are reported to be illiterate. This situation is due to lack of awareness among the tribal communities about the schemes of state and central governments for providing free education to the tribal boys and girls.

6. The problem of poverty and unemployment still continue to be alarming in this area. They do not take healthy and nutritional food. Therefore, they always have ill health. So the problem of health of tribal women and girls has been at the crossroads. To overcome the problem of unemployment or underemployment, basic educational facilities along with the vocational guidance and training for development of their skills with a view to improve their potential should be provided.

7. Tribal usually live in inaccessible areas detached from mainstream, often lacking communication facilities and education institutions. Traditional practices like magic and witch craft, preventive technological approaches, poor sanitation, non-utilization of available resources, poverty, illiteracy, poor hygienic and preventive health practices, all comprise to have a detrimental effect on health. Due to poor accessibility both social and physical there is little knowledge about their health practices, health status and prevalent diseases.

8. It was observed during the collection of data a large number of tribal women are unaware of the tribal development programmes of the Union and State

governments. It is therefore. Suggested that these programmes should be spread through visual and print media at large level. In addition the educated young girls from tribal areas should be trained and employed for door-to door propaganda of tribal development schemes of Union and State governments and for giving them proper guidance in seeking benefits from those schemes. Low literacy level of women in the state and the resultant lack of awareness of their rights has made them all the more vulnerable to atrocities. One of the most inhuman and shameful forms of atrocity prevalent in the state is branding a woman as a .witch. and then throwing her out of the society, essentially thrives on illiteracy and ignorance. It is hoped that with the various schemes put in place by the government for educating the tribal girls would achieve desired results. However, the implementation of these schemes needs close monitoring.

9. Majority of the tribal women in the selected research study are interested in organizing self-help groups. Women have opted for schemes like petty trade, vegetable cultivation, horticulture, fishponds, and garment shops through SHGs. Financial assistance from government is required to implement those schemes on an experimental basis. This would boost socio-economic status of these women.

10. Government should also make available adequate grants for education of girl children, health care of girls and pregnant, nursing and old women.

11. To empower women in the state of Jharkhand can be through the participation of women in their own developmental process and decision making with regard to various issues. Sustainable women groups can provide a solution to several other associated gender issues.

12. The micro project should address this issue of creating proper marketing arrangement, market information systems, storage space and minimum processing facilities at the local level. Simple processing activities such as broom making, leaf plate-making, tamarind processing, mat and rope making should be encouraged in the household/cottage sector.

13. ☐Land is the major physical resource available to PTG households. Most of the available land is poor in quality, and there is not very much of it. Agricultural intervention in the form of promoting locally relevant crops, drought resistant crop mix along with the agro forestry should be encouraged. Similarly, horticulture and small irrigation schemes should be encouraged.

14.   The modern medical treatment is accepted if they are efficacious and are available and accessible to PTGs. Actually their resources do not permit them to avail the expensive treatment at distant places. As such the study suggests the strengthening of the local sub-centre and ANMs centers to provide immediate preventive measures at the household level.

15. Reservation for women in political sphere has opened the way to improve the socio-economic status of tribal women. Presently 33% reservation also for women in state and central government employment is an affirmative section. There is a need to build women's capacities through education, organizing self-help groups, arranging economic activities and providing agricultural extension activities. The aim should be to build women's capacities, give information and construct a positive perspective of society. Eradication of illiteracy through education and health care of pregnant and lactating mothers along with newly born babies will have to be clubbed together to successfully impart family planning programmes. Efforts should be made to reduce gap economic and social disparities among tribes.

The overall findings of the study and suggestions described that tribal women or women from any society plays vital roles in the management of household. It can be said that the women shared quiet a significant role of responsibility of running the family. Status of tribal women, their economic right, their participation in management, their chances to employment and food and many other things have been debated for many years, but these issues have not been focused in relation to the tribal women. The few studies of tribal women which have been published have dealt with division of labor, erosion of their status and rights and deterioration in their condition of work. However, the crucial issues facing tribal women have not been pointedly discussed. It is well recognized that the status of tribal women in a tribal society is better than that of their non-tribal counterparts. The sex ratio is favorable, there is no bride burning and there is high participation in economic activities. It is time that the role of tribal women is assessed and the impact on them of growing poverty and deprivation in large areas is particularly highlighted. Women are part of the society and their problems should be treated as society's problems. Women's socio-economic status leads to family emancipation and ultimately emancipation of the country. Thus, efforts should be made to improve women's social, economic and political empowerment.

REFERENCES

Bardhan A.B.,   (1973) :"The Tribal Problem in India", Communist Party of India Publications, New Delhi.

Bailey, F.G.,   (1960) :"Tribe, Caste and Nation", Oxford University Press, Bombay.

Behura, N.K and Panigrahi, N.,   (2006) : "Tribals and the Indian Constitutions", Rawat Publications, New Delhi.

Bakshi, S.R. and Kiran, Bala,   (2000) :"Social and Economic Development of Scheduled Tribes", Deep and Deep Publication Pvt. Ltd, New Delhi.

Barman, Roy,   (1971) :"A Preliminary Appraisal of the Scheduled Tribes of India", Registrar General of India, New Delhi.

Bggichi, T.,   (1994) :"Profile of Some Indian Tribes", Punti Pustak, Callcutta.

Bhange, N.P.,   (1993) :"Tribal Commissions and Committees in India", Himalaya Publishing House, Bombay.

Bhowmik, Sharit J. Kumar,   (1988) :"Development perspective of Tribals", Economic and political Weekly, Vol. xxiii, No. 20, may 14.

Bose, Nirmal Kumar, (1964) :"Change in Tribal Cultures Before and Fter Independence", Man in India,Vol. xxxxiv, No. 10.

Bose, Pradip Kumar, (1981) :"Stratification among Tribals in Gujurat", Economic and Political Weekly, February 7.

Bose, Nirmal Kumar, (1997) :"Some Indian Tribes", National Book Trust, New Delhi.

Bose, Pradip Kumar, (1989) :"The Political Economy of Development in India", Oxford University Press.

Census of India, 2001, 1991, 1981, 1971 and 1961. Registrar General of Census, Government of India, New Delhi.

Chotopadhyaya, 'Kamala Devi, (1979) :"Tribalism in India", Vikas Publishing House, New Delhi.

Chattopadhyaya, K.P., (1949):"The Tribal problem and its solution", Eastern Anthropology, Vol. viii, No. 1.

D.N. Majumdar,   (1961) :"Races and Cultures of India", Asia Publishing House, Bombay.

Danda, A.K.,   (1991) :"Tribal Economy in India", Inter-India Publications: New Delhi.

Dash Sharma, P.,   (2006) :"Anthropology of primitive tribes in India", Serials publication, New Delhi.

Dutta, Tara,	(2001) :"Tribal Development in India", Gyna Publishing House, Dew Delhi.
Danda, A.K.,	(1988) :"Tribes in India", man in India, Vol. iv.
Dixit, K.Nishi,	(2006) :"Tribals in India", Vista international Publishing house, New Delhi.
Deoogankar, S.G.,	(1980) :"Problems of Development of Tribal Areas", Leeladevi Publications, New Delhi.
Deoogankar, S.G.,	(1992) :"Tribal Development Plans, Implementation and Evaluation", Concept Publishing Company.
Devendra, Thacker,	(1986) :"Socio-economic Development of Tribes in India", Deep and Deep Publications, New Delhi.
Dubey, S.C.,	(1990) :"Traditions and Development", Vikas Publishing House, PVT. Ltd., New Delhi.
Dubey, S.C.,	(1960) :"Approaches to the Tribal Problem in India", (edited by L.P. Vidyarthi), Indian Anthropology in Action, Ranchi.
Furer, Haimendorf,	(1982) :"Tribes of India", Oxford University Press, Bombay.
Ghurye, G.S.,	(1963) :"The Scheduled Tribes", Popular Prakashan, Bombay.
Government of India,	(2001) :"Working group for Empowering Scheduled Tribes during the Tenth Five Year Plan", Ministry of Tribal Affairs, New Delhi.
Hasnain, Nadeem,	(1999) :"Planned Development Among Tribals", Rawat Publications, New Delhi.
Hasnain, Nadeem,	(1996) :"Tribal Development Schemes: An Evalluation", Shakti Publishers, Udaipur.
Kamaladevi, Chotopadhyaya,	(1978) :'Tribalism in India', Deep and Deep Publication, New Delhi, p. 1.
Kunhaman, M.,	(1989) :"Development of Tribal Economy", Classical Publishing Company, New Delhi.
Ministry of Tribal Affaires,	(2008) :"Annual Report 2007-08", Government of Indian, New Delhi.
Majumdar, D.N. and Madan, T.N.,	(1956) :"An Introduction to Social Anthropology", Asia Publishing House, Bombay.
Majumdar, D.N.,	(1937) :"A Tribe in Transition: A Study of Cultural Pattern", London.
Majumdar, D.N.,	(1937) ;"A Tribe in Transition: A study in Cultural Pattern", Longmans Green and Company, London.

Majumdar, D.N.,   (1950) :"Affairs of Tribe: A Study in Tribal Dynamics", Universal Publishers, New Delhi.

Majumdar, D.N.,   (1961) :"Races and Culture of India", Asia Publishing House, Bombay.

Majumdar, D.N.,   (1963) :"Fortunes of Primitive Tribes", The Universal Publishers, Ltd., Lucknow.

Mehta Prakash Chandra, (2000) :"Tribal Development in 20th century", Durga Taldar Shiva Publishers, Udaipur.

Mohanty, P.K.,   (2002) :"Development of Primitive Tribal Groups in India", Kalpaz Publications, Delhi.

Man Das Gupta,   (1984) :"Tribal unrest", Economic and political Weekly, March 17.

Prakash, Chandra Mehta, (2000) :"Tribal Development in 20th Century", Shiva Publishers and Distributors, Udaipur.

Pati, R.N. and Jagannath Dash, (2002) :"Tribal and Indigenous people of India: problems and prospects", APH publishing corporation, New Delhi.

Pati, R.N. and Dash, J., (2002) :"Tribal and Indigenous People of India: Problems and Prospects", New Delhi, APH.

Prasad, R.R.,   (1988) :"Tribal Development in India, Strategies and Programmes", Journal of Rural Development, Vol. vii, No. 1, January.

Remamani, V.S.,   (1988) :"Tribal Economy Problems and Prospects", Chough Publications, Allahabad.

Roy Burman, B.K.,   (1960) :"Basic Concept of Tribal Welfare and Integration", (edited by L.P. Vidyarthi), Indian Anthropology in Action, Ranchi University Press, Ranchi.

Roy Burman, B.K.,   (1997) :"Tribal and Indigenous people: A Global Overview", The Eastern Anthropologist, Vol. 50, No. 1, pp17-26.

Roy Burman, B.K.,   (1969) :"Some dimensions of Transformation of Tribal Society in India", Journal of Social Research, Vol. xi, NO. 1.

Sahay, Shushma Prasad, (1988) :"Tribal Women Labours: Aspects of Economic and Physical Exploitation", Gyan Publishing House, New Delhi.

Sahu, Chaturbhuj,   (2006) :"Aspects of Tribal Studies" Sarup and Sons publication, New Delhi.

Saxena, N.C.,	(1995) :"Forests, People and Profit: New Equations for Sustainability", Natraj Publishers, Dehradun
Sharma, B.D.,	(1975) :"Tribal Development- A Brief Review", Tribal Research and Development Institute, Bhopal.
Singh, K.S.,	(1994) :"The Scheduled Tribes", Vol. III. Oxford University Press, Delhi.
Singh, K.,	(1982) :"Economics of Tribes and their Transformation", Concept Publishing House, New Delhi.
Singh, Suresh,	(1981) :"Tribal Situation in India", Biblio impex Publishers, New Delhi.
Tripathy, S.N.,	(1999) :"Tribals in Transition", Discovery Publishing House, New Delhi.
Vidyarthi, L.P.,	(1981) :"Tribal Development and its Administration", Concept Publishing Company, New Delhi.

Vidyarthi, L.P. and Rai, B.K., (2000):"The Tribal Culture of India", Concept Publishing Company, New Delhi.

Bibliography

Abraham, Francis.	2000	: Modern Sociological Theory. Calcutta: Oxford University Press.
Ahmad, Aijazuddin & Raza Moonic	1990	: An Aatlas of Tribal of India. New Delhi: Concept Publishing Company.
Ahuja, D. R.	1980	: Folklore of Rajasthan. Delhi: National book Trust.
Alexander, K. C.	1981	: Peasant Organizations in South India. Delhi: Indian Social Institute.
Ambastha, N. K.,	1969	: Critical Study of Tribal Education. Delhi: S. Chand N.
Best, W. John.	1982	: Research Agencies in Education. New Delhi: Prentice Hall of India Pvt. Ltd.
Bhatti S H.	2000	: Folk Religion: change and continuity. Rawat Publication.
Bisht, S. B.	2001	: Ethnography of a Tribe. New Delhi: Rawat Pub.
Bose, N. K.	1972	: Some Indian Tribes. Delhi: Nat Book Trust.
Bose, N. K.	1971	: Tribal Life in India. India the Land the People Delhi: Nat Book Trust.
Burnett, David.	1988	: Unearthly powers. East Bourne: MARC,
Channa C. M. (Ed)	2004	: Encyclopaedia of Indian Tribes & Castes. New Delhi: Cosmo Publication.
Craib, Ian.	1997	: Classical Social Theory. New York: Oxford University Press.
Chattophadiyaya, K.,	1978	: Tribalism in India. Delhi. Vikas.
Denis Coelho (Ed)	1995	: Changing Perspectives in Education. New Delhi: India Social Institute Publication.
Donovan, O Wilbur.	1996	:Biblical Charistianity in African Perspective. London: the Paternoster Press.
Dube, S. C. ed.	1977	: Tribal Heritage of India. Delhi: Vikas
Emory, William.	1976	: Business Researcher methods, IIlinois: Richard D. Irwin. Inc,

Furer- Haimendorf, C. von 1982: Tribes of India: the Struggle for Survival. Delhi. O.U.P.

Furer- Haimendorf, C. von 1979: South Indian Societies: A Study of Values and Social Control. Delhi: Sterling Pubs.

Ghurge S, G.	1995	: The Scheduled Tribe. Bombay: Popular Prakashan.
Gehman, J. Richard.	1989	: African Traditional Religion in Biblical Perspectives, Kenya: Kesho Pub.
Georg Pfefer (Ed.)	1997	: Contemporary Society Tribal Studies. New Delhi:

Goode, W. J. and Hatt P. K. 1952   : Methods in social research. New York: Mc Graw Hill Book Co..

Haralambos. M.   2003   : Sociology themes and Perspectives. New Delhi: Oxford University Press.

Hinnells R John.   1991   : A Handbook of Living Religiopns. Middlesex: Penguin Books.

Hrangkhuma F.   2004   : Tribes in Transition. Bangalore. SAIACS Press.

Kingslay Davis.   1998   : Human Society. New Delhi: perfect Publications.

Kulirani, B. Francis, 1984   : Ethnography Structure and Process: The Paniyan of Wayanad (unpublished monograph) Anthropological Survey of India, Mysore.

Jha, Makhan.   1999   : An Introduction to Social Anthropology. New Delhi: Vikas publishing House.

Locke, Rona and Trevor.   1992   : Tribal for Christ, Bangalore: Outreach Publications IEM.

Longchar, Wati A.   1991   : The Tribal Religious Traditions. Jorhat: India, Eastern Theological College.

Majumdar, D. N.   1973   :Races and Culture of India. Asia Publishing House Bombay:

Manorama Sharma,   2004   : Folk India, New Delhi: Sandeep Prakashan.

Mann, R. S. ed.   1981   : Nature- Man- Spirit Complex in Tribal India. Delhi: Concept Publisher.

Mann, R. S.   1996   : Aspects of Indian Social Anthropology. New Delhi: Concept Publishing Company.

Mark K. C.   1984   : The Church in India: His Mission Tomorrow.

Mukhi. R H.   1999   : Principle of Sociology. Delhi: S. B. D. Publishers and Distributors.

Nair, Gopalan. C.   1911   :Wayanad its People and Traditions. New Delhi: Asian Educational Service.

Negi S B.   2000   :Social Anthropology. A case study of India. New Delhi: Kedar Nath.

Nehru, S.   1971   : The Discovery of India. London: Merridian Bks.

Nettur P. Damodaran 1974   : Adivasikalude Keralam (Malayalam). NBS Kottayam.

Parthasarathy, Jekka. 2007   : Education and Development Among the Tribes Udhangamangalam. Tribal Research Centre. Govt. of T. N.

Paula Muni, Lakra.   2000   : Tribal India Communities Customs and Culture New Delhi Dominant Publishers and Distributers.

Saravanavel P.   1999   : Research Methodology. New Delhi: Kitab Mahal.

Shan, M A.   1996   : Social Structure and Change. New Delhi: SAGE Pub.

Sharma, Nath, Ram.	1987	: Social Anthropology and Indian Tribes. Bombay: Media Promoters & Publishing.
Shiv. R. Metha.	1984	: Rural Development Policies and Programs- A Sociological Perspective. Sage Publications. New Delhi.
Singh, Yogendra.	2000	: Culture Change in India. New Delhi: Rawat Publications
Singh, S.	1972	: Tribal Situation in India. Simla Indian Institute of Advanced Studies.
Singh K. S	1995	: People of India Vol. XXVIII Part. III. New Delhi Anthropological Survey of India Pub.
Singh K.	1990	: Social Change in India. Lucknow: Prakashan Kendra Publishing.
Srinivas, M. N.	1966	: Social Change in Modern India. Delhi: Orient Longman.
Stephen M.	1999	: A Liberated Vission. Delhi: ISPCK Publishing.
Subramanya G,	2003	: Social Problems with special reference to India. Bangalore Sapna Book House.
Sunder Raj.	1986	:The Confusion Called Conversion. New Delhi: TRACI Publication.
Topro R. S.	2000	: Tribes in India. Delhi: Indian Pub. Distributors.
Thomas M. M.	1965	: Awakening. Bangalore: Christian Institute for the Study of Religion and society.
Tiwari, Kumar, Shiv. House.	1994	: Encyclopaedia of Indian Tribals Vol. 1 Delhi Rahul Publishing
Vatsyayan,	1998	: Anthropology: Social and Culture. Delhi Kedae Nath Ram Nath.
Young P, V.	1982	: Scientific Social Survey and Research. New Delhi: Prentice Hall of India.

www.ingramcontent.com/pod-product-compliance
Lightning Source LLC
Chambersburg PA
CBHW050116280326
41933CB00010B/1131